The SOUL of a
PILgrim

"This creative, moving book beckons the pilgrim into the inner journey through daily life. Deeply grounded in creative spiritual practices, it is both a guidebook and an inspiration."

Sheryl A. Kujawa-Holbrook
Author of *Pilgrimage—The Sacred Art*

"Of all the books that Christine Paintner has written, this is by far my personal favorite. To refer to it as a comprehensive manual for the journey doesn't do justice to the incredible richness of its resources. It definitely reawakened the inner pilgrim in me!"

Wil Hernandez, Obl. O.S.B.
Founder and Executive Director
CenterQuest.org

"Making our own pilgrimage to the heart inside our heart is perhaps the most challenging and yet most rewarding journey we can make. *The Soul of a Pilgrim* is the perfect companion to have in our pocket along the way."

Bruce Davis
Retreat Leader
SilentStay.com

"Christine Valters Paintner and her husband John beckon the reader toward a transformative way of pilgrimage. Poetry, practices, and midrash weave this wisdom into daily life."

Mary C. Earle
Author of *Marvelously Made: Gratefulness and the Body*

"Christine Valters Paintner's latest work is an invitation to take leave of the familiar and go on pilgrimage—not necessarily by traveling abroad, but by simplifying one's life, letting go of pre-conceived and perhaps deeply rooted notions, and opening oneself up to the Spirit of wisdom in one's heart. Complemented by the scriptural reflections of her husband, John, and her own creative poetry, this marvelous book takes the reader on a journey of discovery that can profoundly change the direction of one's life."

Edward C. Sellner
Author of *Pilgrimage: Exploring a Great Spiritual Practice*

The SOUL of a PILGRIM

Eight Practices for the Journey Within

CHRISTINE VALTERS PAINTNER

With Biblical Reflections by John Valters Paintner

SORIN BOOKS NOTRE DAME, INDIANA

© 2015 by Christine Valters Paintner

All rights reserved. No part of this book may be used or reproduced in any manner whatsoever, except in the case of reprints in the context of reviews, without written permission from Sorin Books®, P.O. Box 428, Notre Dame, IN 46556-0428, 1-800-282-1865.

www.sorinbooks.com

Paperback: ISBN-13 978-1-933495-86-6

E-Book: ISBN-13 978-1-933495-87-3

Cover image © Thinkstock.com.

Cover and text design by Brian C. Conley.

Printed and bound in the United States of America.

Library of Congress Cataloging-in-Publication Data
Paintner, Christine Valters.
  The soul of a pilgrim : eight practices for the journey within : / Christine Valters Paintner ; with biblical reflections by John Valters Paintner.
    pages cm
  Includes bibliographical references and index.
  ISBN 978-1-933495-86-6 (alk. paper) -- ISBN 1-933495-86-3 (alk. paper)
  1. Christian pilgrims and pilgrimages. 2. Spiritual life--Christianity. I. Title.
BV5067.P35 2015
263'.041--dc23
                    2014049245

To my beloved husband, John, with whom I just celebrated twenty years of marriage, one of the greatest journeys of my life.

HOW TO BE a PILGRIM

Air travel is like
ancient pilgrims walking on their
knees, flight delays and narrow seats
offer their own kind of penance.

You jettison excess baggage,
leaving behind the heavy makeup case,
knowing the rain will
wash you free of artifice.

Books you wanted to carry left too,
no more outside words needed,
then go old beliefs which keep
you taut and twisted inside.

Blistered feet stumble over rocky
fields covered with wildflowers and you
realize this is your life,
full of sharp stones and color.

Red-breasted robins call forth
the song already inside,
a hundred griefs break open under
dark clouds and downpour.

Rise and fall of elation and exhaustion,
the tides a calendar of unfolding,
a bright star rises and you remember
a loved one waiting miles away.

A new hunger is kindled by the sight of
cows nursing calves in a field,
spying a spotted pony, you forget
the weight and seriousness of things.

Salmon swim across the Atlantic,
up the River Corrib's rapids to the
wide lake, and you wonder if you have

also been called here for death and birth.

This is why we journey:
to retrieve our lost intimacy with the world,
every creature a herald of poems
that sleep in streams and stones.

"Missing you" scrawled on a postcard sent home,
but you don't follow with
"wish you were here."
This is a voyage best made alone.

contents

INTRODUCTION

*To journey without being changed is to be a nomad. To change
without journeying is to be a chameleon. To journey and be
transformed by the journey is to be a pilgrim.*

—**Mark Nepo**, *The Exquisite Risk*

*Ideally, a human life should be a constant pilgrimage of dis-
covery. The most exciting discoveries happen at the frontiers.
When you come to know something new, you come closer to
yourself and to the world. Discovery enlarges and refines your
sensibility. When you discover something, you transfigure
some of the forsakenness of the world.*

—**John O'Donohue**, *Eternal Echoes*

PILGRIMAGE AS INNER AND OUTER JOURNEY

The Hebrew and Christian Scriptures are filled with journeys. Adam
and Eve are sent forth from Paradise into the world. Abraham and Sarah are called away from the land which was familiar. Moses and Miriam
lead the Israelites out of slavery in Egypt. Mary and Joseph seek a place
to give birth. The Prodigal Son leaves home and returns. The Samaritan
woman walks from her own brokenness to the living water. Jesus makes
his final journey to Jerusalem accompanied by his disciples. The two
disciples on the road to Emmaus are joined by an unexpected guest on
their road. All of these stories hold mysteries for us to explore.

Journeys are movements from one place to another, often to a
place that is unfamiliar, foreign, and strange. In fact, the Latin root
of the word pilgrimage, *peregrini*, means "strange" or "stranger." The

1

journey to become a pilgrim means becoming a stranger in the service of transformation.

A pilgrimage is an intentional journey into this experience of unknowing and discomfort for the sake of stripping away preconceived expectations. We grow closer to God beyond our own imagination and ideas.

In recent years, there has been a reclaiming of the practice of pilgrimage that flourished in the Middle Ages. People of all religious traditions are flocking to many sites of spiritual significance. Christians are walking to Marian sites like Lourdes and Medjugorje. Muslims circle the Hajarul Aswad (the black stone) in Mecca. Hindus travel to bathe in the sacred river. Safe to say, journeys to find spiritual knowledge are hardwired into the human experience.

In the spring of 2012, my husband, John, and I embarked on our own great pilgrimage. For several years, we traveled to Europe on ancestral pilgrimages to Ireland and England, the land of our mothers' ancestors. On other trips, we ventured to Germany, Austria, and Latvia, the land of our fathers' ancestors. These journeys helped us to reconnect with the landscapes and cultures of our ancestors. As we walked in the pathways of those who came before us, their blood beat in our veins as we gloried in the beauty around us.

After those adventures, a number of shifts happened in our lives to open the way for a more radical journey. We experienced a call to sell or give away everything we owned—home, car, furniture, books, belongings—and board a ship to cross the Atlantic Ocean.

Two years before this midlife journey, I sought to file the paper work to reclaim my citizenship in Austria. My father remained an Austrian citizen his entire life even as he raised me in New York. His love of his home country drew me to complete the circle. This became an open door to our great adventure.

John and I had been drawn to the idea of living overseas for some time. We knew there was a different mindset in Europe. People seemed to rush less and enjoy their lives more. They did less shopping at big box stores and supported their local markets. We were drawn to becoming strangers in these places, not just for a few weeks of summer travel but to see what we might discover about ourselves. We wanted our own assumptions and expectations challenged.

John had taught high school for twelve years and felt ready for a break even though he still loved the Hebrew Scriptures, his primary subject matter. An upcoming significant change in the curriculum at the school where he taught prompted us to consider a new stage in our lives.

I believe in taking physical pilgrimages to faraway places. I know the value of stepping into foreign cultures and illuminating all the expectations I hold about how life should work. I will share many of these discoveries in the chapters ahead.

I also believe that pilgrimage is very much an inner journey and experience. Many can travel long distances and take a lot of pictures. They see things through the lens of a tourist and not through the eyes of a pilgrim.

Some may not travel long distances on the outside. The inside, however, is another matter. These pilgrims travel long, arduous, and soul-altering distances. When they do, they are transformed in rewarding and profound ways.

When we take inward and outward journeys, we can be pilgrims as long as we stay open to new experiences. We must always be mindful that pilgrimage is an outer journey that serves our inner transformation.

I love the impulse to experience the horizon-broadening adventure of travel and the invitation of pilgrimage to go to unexplored places. The purpose of these voyages, however, is always to return home carrying the new insight back to everyday life.

SIT IN YOUR CELL

There is a story from Abba Moses, one of the Desert Fathers, who when asked by a new monk for a word replied: "Sit in your cell and your cell will teach you everything."

Desert wisdom reminds me that my monk's cell, which is really a metaphor for the inner cell of my heart, is the place I am called to sit and be present in the moment. When I do, I discover the mystery of myself and of God. This is the place of the holiest of pilgrimages.

Pilgrimage is an archetypal experience, meaning that the metaphor of journey for the spiritual life is found across time and traditions. Is

there a greater adventure than plunging into our own depths and un-
covering what the mystics have told us for centuries: the heart of God
beating within our own? Pilgrimage calls us to be attentive to the divine
at work in our lives through deep listening, patience, opening ourselves
to the gifts that arise in the midst of discomfort, and going out to our
own inner wild edges to explore new frontiers.

This is a perilous journey because I encounter my own shadowy
places. Their resistance draws strength out of the small and hurting
pockets of my soul. The only way I can sustain this inner gaze is to kneel
down at the altar and surrender to the arms of the Holy One. When I do,
my dark places are transformed into wisdom and grace. Each moment
I am called to awaken to this journey within. No passport is necessary.

This book invites you on an inner pilgrimage. Creative expression
and contemplation will be our practices to help us navigate. Our focus will be on the expressive arts where we engage the process over the
product and our creativity helps to illumine our inner landscape.

*Pause just a moment and reconnect with the longing that brought you
here to this time and experience. How might you honor that longing in the
season ahead?*

OVERVIEW OF THE BOOK

This book is structured around eight central spiritual practices which
are key to experiencing pilgrimage in our daily lives. In chapter 1 we
explore the call that sets us out on our journey. Sometimes this is a welcome summons, and sometimes life forces us onto a journey we would
rather not take. Chapter 2 invites us to consider what we need to bring
with us for the journey. Pilgrimage invites us to a radical simplicity, to
not be weighed down by too many things, attitudes, and beliefs that
stand in the way of going somewhere new.

In chapter 3 we consider the thresholds that pilgrimage is inviting us
to cross. Journeys call us across borders. Thresholds are liminal places
where we release the old and the new has not yet come into fullness. The
ancient Celts called these "thin places" where heaven and earth came
close. Chapter 4 introduces the idea of making the way by walking,
which means to let go of our maps, plans, and guidebooks. We are to

enter into a radical trusting of the Spirit. Pilgrimage calls us to yield our own agendas and follow where we are being led.

As I mentioned at the beginning, the root of the word for pilgrim means "stranger." Along with becoming the stranger, pilgrimage invites us to embrace being uncomfortable. Going beyond the edges of our sense of security stretches us in new ways, breaking us open. When this happens, something unexpected will walk through that open door. This is the theme for chapter 5.

Chapter 6 reminds us that the pilgrim is always starting. The idea is rooted in monastic tradition. It holds us to the concept that we are human and will stumble along the way. Beginning again demands humility and an openness to conversion. We acknowledge that for all of our lives we are beginners at the spiritual path.

Chapter 7 asks us to go deeper than just being uncomfortable. Pilgrimage calls us to a radical sense of mystery. God works in ways we don't understand. We encounter synchronicities along the way. We have to release our goals and hopes for what the end of the journey will look like.

Finally, in chapter 8 pilgrimage leads us back home again, transformed by what we have experienced. The gift of the journey is always meant to return us to ourselves with new vision and the commitment to bring what we have discovered back to our communities.

Each chapter offers reflections on these themes. They include a scripture story to break open the theme further, an invitation to the practice of lectio divina, and creative exploration through photography. After this contemplation, you'll be invited to write your own Midrash, an ancient Jewish practice, as a way of entering into the story and finding your own journey.

I am also delighted to include a scripture reflection in each chapter written by my husband, John. He has a great love for the wisdom and insight these stories can provide for our own journeys, a love cultivated by teaching sacred scripture to high schoolers.

WORKING WITH THIS BOOK

Just about every book I have written has been about process, which means they aren't meant to be read all at once. You might be exploring pilgrimage as a theme in daily life. You might be preparing for an up-coming physical journey, or perhaps you have been thrust into a new season of life through a crisis point like a loss of a job. There might be a sense of a deeper invitation at work. If you seek to view this unintended journey through the lens of pilgrimage, depth and meaning might be added to the experience.

I encourage you to linger over each chapter and do the inner work it suggests. Gather with a small group and meet weekly, to share and discuss the ideas in each chapter. Allow time for integration of what you are discovering.

HOW TO create a retreat in everyday life

Set Aside Time

First, take a few moments before you begin to name a commitment that feels accessible for your life. Go through your calendar and mark off the times when you want to dedicate yourself to reflection and creating.[1]

My suggestion is to commit to at least twenty to thirty minutes each day of quiet reflection and a longer period of two to three hours each week for a mini-retreat in which you engage some of the creative explo-rations. Reflect on the movements of your journey. If this is not possible in your life, allow what can be managed. Do not shut off the journey before you even begin. Even a small period of time each week can begin to plant seeds.

Create Space

Second, find a space in your home that you can bless as your retreat space. It might just be a cozy chair in the corner of your bedroom and a small folding table where you can lay out your journal. You might already have a prayer space in your home. Dedicate this space to the journey ahead. Perhaps include a candle and small altar space with a meaningful symbol or two.

Begin with Meditation

As you get ready to embark on this inner pilgrimage, I invite you to meditate and get in touch with your own deepest longings. Allow this contemplation to guide you as you think about the time commitment you want to make.

Begin by allowing a few moments to sink into the stillness. Deepen your breath and bring it down into your belly so that you feel your belly expanding with each inhale. Allow the exhale to be long and slow. Imagine as you breathe in that you are receiving the gift of life which sustains you moment by moment even when you are completely unaware of it. As you exhale, imagine that you are releasing, letting go of whatever is not needed for this time, anything that might be keeping you from being fully present.

Become aware of your body and notice if there are any places of tightness or holding. Bring your breath to those tight places to help soften and release.

See if you can draw your awareness with your breath from your head down to your heart center, placing a hand on your heart to make a physical connection. Rest there a moment and just notice what you are experiencing without trying to change it. See if you can be with your feelings without judgment, bringing compassion to wherever you find yourself right now. Remember what the mystics across traditions tell us about the infinite source of compassion which dwells in our hearts. Breathe in that compassion.

In your imagination, see yourself at a doorway. Spend some time being with the door and noticing its qualities. What are the colors and textures? Is it old or new? Is it worn with time or shiny? Is it closed or slightly ajar? See if you can be with whatever image comes to mind without trying to change it.

Imagine yourself pausing here, knowing that as you cross this threshold you enter into a liminal kind of time, *kairos* as the ancients called it. This is time outside of time, where you will encounter both challenges and grace along the way. In threshold space you are in between, you are invited to rest into unknowing—about what the journey will bring, about even where you are going exactly.

Notice what you are carrying with you and see if there is anything you can set aside before you begin this journey. What you are carrying might be objects and possessions. They might also be beliefs or attitudes about yourself, life, or God. What could you set down on the ground and leave for this time? What are the essentials that you want to have with you? What feels important to carry?

When you feel ready, open the door and step across the threshold. Pause there on the other side. What do you see? Taste? Smell? Feel? Hear? Allow yourself some time to just be with whatever felt experience arises.

Stand here for a while, taking in the full spectrum of what you are feeling. Welcome in joy, excitement, fear, trepidation, anxiety, and whatever else is arising with an open heart. Call on that compassion once again.

Offer a prayer here at the threshold for whatever your heart's desire is for this time ahead. Speak from your heart about whatever it is you long for most. Make a commitment to continue showing up to the practice and to return ever so gently when you fall away.

Remember this place, knowing that you will be journeying forward from here into unknown territory. Know that you have everything you need to navigate this time ahead. Feel the community of fellow pilgrims across the world as guides and companions.

When you feel ready, gently deepen your breathing once again and bring your awareness from this inner space to the world around you once again. Allow some time for journaling and reflection on your experience. Name the images that arose for you.

Receive a Seven-Word Prayer

As a way of naming the grace you seek for this time, I invite you to open yourself to receive a seven-word prayer to carry with you. Just notice what the prayer of your heart is for this time and what words or images seem to draw you forward. Seven is a sacred number in religious traditions and also requires that you return to the essence of what you long for. No extraneous words necessary. Let this evolve over several days, sitting with whether the words that have emerged feel right for you.

Once it has landed, offered a sense of rightness in your being, let this be your mantra for the time ahead. Much like praying with prayer beads or a holy word in centering prayer, the mantra can be a focus and its repetition a source of comfort. Repeat it gently to yourself several times during the day. Consider writing it in your journal and maybe on a sticky note by your computer or on your mirror so it greets you each day. Say it in moments of transition from one activity to another for these are threshold spaces, times which are especially ripe for leaning into sacred awareness.

Anoint Yourself for Pilgrimage

Anointing is an ancient practice of honoring transition times in life. We can practice anointing of ourselves as a way of celebrating our life journeys and what our dreams are for the time ahead.

Gather some carrier oil (like jojoba or almond) scented with essential oils. You can purchase a blend you like in a health food store or you can purchase the carrier oil and essential oils separately so that you can blend your own. I especially love lavender, rose otto, and neroli, but let your nose lead you in discerning which fragrances bless your journey best. Pour a little into a small bowl. Dip your fingers in and begin to bless the different parts of your body.

> Feet—bless your feet, asking that they might carry you forward in this season to new possibilities
>
> Hands—bless your hands, asking that they might help you to give form to creative expressions
>
> Heart—bless your heart, asking that it be open to wonder and numinous moments
>
> Throat—bless your throat, asking that you gain courage to speak your truth
>
> Lips—bless your lips, asking that you take in that which is most nourishing
>
> Third eye—bless your third eye (middle of your forehead), asking that intuition and the wisdom of dreams help to guide you.

Blessings on the journey ahead!

Chapter 1

THE PRACTICE OF HEARING THE CALL AND RESPONDING

*And it was then that in the depths of sleep
Someone breathed to me: "You alone can do it,
Come immediately."*

—Jules Supervielle, "The Call"

HEARING THE CALL AND SAYING YES

This is the beauty of the pilgrim journey. All of us are called. When you read the description of this book you felt it: a sense of calling that stirred a longing in you and compelled you to make a commitment.

We are brought into the world with what many indigenous cultures call "original medicine." This means that we are unique creations. We've never been in the past and won't be in the future. No one carries the same combination of gifts, talents, resources, opportunities, and challenges. This unique alchemy is our "original medicine." St. Ignatius of Loyola, a sixteenth-century mystic, said that the deepest desires of our heart are planted by God.

"Medicine" is not just referring to a healing balm or potion. Our unique abilities contain our power to act in the world. They enable us to explore, discover, express, and heal. Our original medicine emerges from our "true self." Thomas Merton, in *New Seeds of Contemplation*, describes this concept as our deepest selves when we have stripped away self-deception, self-criticism, self-inflation, masks, expectations, and judgments:

> For me to be a saint means to be myself. Therefore the problem of sanctity and salvation is in fact the problem of finding out who I am and of discovering my true self. God leaves us free to be whatever we like. We can be ourselves or not, as we please. We are at liberty to be real, or to be unreal. We may be true or false, the choice is ours. We may wear now one mask and now another, and never, if we so desire, appear with our own true face. [1]

There is a mystery here because you can't arrive at this discovery overnight. We must journey for a lifetime to discover our deepest and most mysterious talents. However, there is a paradox that comes with these realizations. While we must venture far to find our "true self," it is also always with us. We must continue to learn how to let go of what is false in our lives. We must throw out what keeps us from offering our own healing balm to the world. The more we live from this awareness the more our gifts can bring peace and joy to others.

This call to embark on a rigorous journey of reclaiming ourselves and our relationship to the divine often comes without our bidding. There are many reasons we might begin an inner pilgrimage. Perhaps we've experienced a great loss: a job, our health, a dear friend, a sense of identity, financial security, or a marriage. We know we can't return to life as usual. That way is now closed. This is the call to which we must respond. If we say no, it means numbing ourselves and living in denial of this great shifting we've experienced. When we say yes, it means to acknowledge that even our moments of profound sorrow can lead us to renewed vision and life.

our own Annunciations

The feast of the Annunciation remembers Mary's own pilgrim journey of saying "yes." She walked into the unknown with only her trust in God to carry her. Anyone can identify with Mary and her questions. She shows perfect humanness when she asks Gabriel, "How can this be?" when he tells her she will be with child.

The angel explains and she answers, "Here I am." What we are not told in the story is the long interior journey of the heart Mary went through before she said yes. This is where our imagination must enter the story and make it our own.

I like to imagine that during the months before the angel appeared, Mary felt restless, unsettled and a sense that something was ripening within her. This is how a sense of calling often emerges. We ponder for a long time the possibilities, and weigh the options. We calculate the pros and cons. We consider the contingencies.

If we pay attention to our inner life, when the angel finally arrives (and she may be wearing a multitude of disguises as angels can be tricky that way) we might suddenly recognize that the invitation they are offering meets us exactly where we are. The "yes" we've been resisting for so long suddenly slides off the tongue with ease, grace, and astonishment. Sometimes the "yes" is still a struggle as we might still feel uncertain and tentative. Yet, somehow, the drive to act compels us forward because we can't help it.

We don't often think about what Mary went through after she said yes. I imagine that in the days following her profound answer, she still struggled as she faced the ramifications of her decisions. I'm sure she felt the sheer excitement at being full of new life and some genuine anxiety over what this new birth would cost her, what possible drawbacks would enter her life.

There are so many beautiful depictions in art of this moment from scripture. Masters of artistic expression show us the angel and Mary facing one another. If the artist has done their job, you can feel the anticipation and trembling. We see the majesty and the intimacy of the moment. They are talking like two created beings. He is asking and she is consenting. There are no demands.

Consider the angels of annunciation in your own lifetime. When have they arrived? What form did they take? Are they human, animal, tree, ocean wave, crow, spirit voice? Allow some space to honor all the ways you've been asked to give your consent to being filled with possibility. Hold to the times you've said yes and no. Be gentle with both, and trust each response contains its own kind of grace.

Pilgrimage of the Art-Making Process

*People travel to wonder at the height of mountains, at huge
waves of the sea, at the long courses of rivers, at the vast*

compass of the ocean, at the circular motion of the stars . . .
and they pass by themselves without wondering.

—St. Augustine, *Confessions*

I long for You so much
I have even begun to travel
Where I have never been before.

—Hafiz, *The Subject Tonight Is Love*

Pilgrimage calls us to go where, as Hafiz says, we've never been before. We might discover this truth in our inner and outer journeys.

The daily practice of making art is one way of growing more intimate with our inner life. We become more curious about what is stirring inside our heart. Creative practice can raise our resistance, our blocks, and our inner demons. We should see this as a part of the process as we get to know ourselves on a deeper level.

Consider your art-making time as a meditation practice where the only "goal" is to be aware of the voices inside you, especially the critical ones. Notice what they have to say and then gently return to your practice. Over time you will discover that these voices of judgment and insecurity are the same ones that rise up and undermine you in everyday life. Art becomes a place where we can grow familiar with them and dive into our inner life despite their distraction. It also becomes a place to welcome in the voices of joy and ease and recognize the things that make our hearts delight.

As we work in the expressive arts, we're invited to place emphasis on the *creative process* over the artistic *product*. We live in a very product-oriented culture. The way we spend our time may only seem valuable if we have something to show for it. That is, if we are productive and "busy." We often measure our own worth by how much we accomplish in a given time and how many goals we reach.

In the expressive arts however, as in prayer, the focus is on the *process* of creativity itself rather than creating a beautiful product. If we do so, the art created will be beautiful through an authentic expression of the soul. The heart of the work is to free ourselves from the expectations and goals. They can keep us from entering deeply into our own creative longings and expression.

One of the metaphors I use in teaching the expressive arts is *pilgrimage*. On a pilgrimage, as in art-making, we take a journey to encounter the sacred within ourselves in a more intimate way. We prepare for the art-making time with prayer and take only the essential tools. Pilgrims bring an intention for the journey. This intention is an essential element for making the time of creating art an act of prayer. In the process we are invited to be fully present to each moment as it unfolds.

On pilgrimage, as in the art-making process, we risk entering the unknown with the hope of being transformed. We leave our familiar world behind. We are also connected to a whole community of people who have taken this journey before us, those who travel alongside of us, and those who will in the future. The journey transforms us so we may be ready for our destination. We are transformed in the process of the creative act and are allowing ourselves to be led through the experience by the divine impulse. This changes us on the inside and the outside.

Art-making as pilgrimage helps us to understand the arts as a *process of discovery* about ourselves and about God. When we enter the creative process with the intention of listening for the movements of the Spirit, we discover new insights about ourselves and God.

We will be working with two art mediums primarily on this journey: photography as a contemplative practice and Midrash as a creative engagement with scripture texts. More details about these a little further on in the chapter.

SPIRITUAL PRACTICE AS DAILY PILGRIMAGE

> *What nine months of attention does for an embryo*
> *forty early mornings will do*
> *for your gradually growing wholeness.*
>
> —**Rumi**, *The Illuminated Rumi*

The poet Rumi reminds us that the continual attention to practice can bring about a holy birthing. Jesus went out into the desert for forty days, called to wrestle with temptation and go deeper into his calling. We are called to this as well. Over the next season we will encounter the temptation to abandon our practice, to leave behind what we experience as life-giving. Be prepared for it to happen often. When this happens make a commitment to return.

In *Wherever You Go, There You Are*, Jon Kabat-Zinn writes that doing yoga and not doing yoga are the same. What he means is that when we return to our practice after having left it for several days (or weeks, months, years) we often have a deeper appreciation for what we neglected. We can come back to our practice with a perspective born of wisdom.

Beginning again is essential. We fall away; we lose our will to persevere for so many reasons. The problem is not with the waning of our inner fire and perseverance. We are human beings and go through times of dryness.

What becomes soul killing is not returning at all. When we realize we have not meditated or created art in days or weeks (or months), our minds have become hard with judgment and self-criticism. We find ourselves even further from the peace than if we just simply return to the practice without anxiety.

Kabat-Zinn also asks, "Can you see that not practicing is an arduous practice?" I believe this means that we each have a life practice, even if it is no practice at all.

These practices can often change us in positive and negative ways. When we have no intentional practice, we might find it difficult to deal with the grief and struggles of life. When pain comes, it might be magnified if we can't center ourselves through intentional practice. Life can become difficult and chaotic, and steal our peace.

Yet, when we cultivate peace in ourselves through art-making, meditation, chanting, yoga, or any number of possible practices, it spills over into the rest of our lives. Intentional practice can anchor us when we are in the middle of the ocean during a hurricane. We can pray with the old Irish fishermen who said, "Oh Lord, your ocean is so big and my boat is so small."

We need practices to act as touchstones so they can sustain us during the journey. They help remind us that the journey will take us beyond our narrow visions and connect with the sacred ground of being. We open our hearts and minds to a more intimate connection to the One who created us and in the process we start to discover our created purpose.

Practices are an essential part of the pilgrim's journey. What practices would support you the most in the season ahead?

What is it that is calling you to this time of pilgrimage? Consider the grace that you seek for the inner journey. Listen for the deep desires of your heart compelling you. When pilgrims left on their journeys they often made a vow of commitment as a way of saying yes. Consider your own vows for this time ahead. What are the practices to which you want to commit?

THE MONK AND PILGRIM DANCE TOGETHER

Isn't it time that your drifting was consecrated into pilgrimage? You have a mission. You are needed. The road that leads to nowhere has to be abandoned. . . . It is a road for joyful pilgrim's intent on the recovery of passion.

—**Alan Jones**, *Passion for Pilgrimage*

This chapter we've listened for our call and prepared ourselves to respond. The story of Adam and Eve opens up possibilities for great pilgrimages that arise from circumstances we would not choose for ourselves. At the same time, we make the choice for the journey to become meaningful and soulful. This second story of creation is about the ways we find ourselves exiled from our heart's home. We all have experiences which leave us feeling far away from ourselves and what is meaningful. Yet the pilgrimage begins when we take responsibility for how we live with this exile, this loss, this rejection. We can continue on in bitterness and longing, or we can choose to live with deepened awareness and commitment to making our way home once again.

We all have an inner pilgrim, and in different seasons this archetype will speak more strongly than others. It calls us out of our comfortable lives into something holy and true. We have an inner monk as well, a part of ourselves that is rooted in ancient practices of listening for another voice to be heard.

The pilgrim in me feels the call of moving outward. My inner pilgrim feels a longing to travel. She wants to walk across new landscapes and find herself a stranger. This helps me release what I know and enter into a deeper truth I can only find when I wander.

Every year, salmon make a long journey from the ocean to the place of their birth. They travel incredible distances as they move upstream. Their inner biological map drive them to the place where they were born.

I know this power. Our inner voice tells us we must leave everything behind and travel to a place we call home. I know the miles of ease and flow. I know the miles of mighty rivers that test my strength and resolve. I know that to refuse this inner longing is to refuse life-giving radiance. Finally, I know that death, the release of things I hold dear, is an essential part of the new birth.

The monk in me feels the call of moving inward. My inner monk knows the deep wisdom to be found in rest, slowness, and spaciousness. I'm tempted to let the productivity of the world make me run faster. The only person who can say "no" and "stop" is me.

I know the power to be gained from following my natural rhythms instead of the rhythms demanded by the world around me. When I'm replenished, my work is sustainable and it gives me joy. When I have joy, I demonstrate to the world how powerful it is to live in this intentional way.

The ancient wisdom of monks has much to offer us on the pilgrim path.

The monk demands obedience to a call. It acts like an invisible thread drawing us forward. Conversion calls for commitment to always being surprised by God. The mysterious thing is that even the monastic call to stability, which usually refers to staying in one place for a lifetime, is an invitation to contemplate life-changing mysteries. When we stay put, we experience all of our own doubts, uncertainties, questions, and judgments. We aren't allowed to run away from the inner challenges of being alive.

We must embrace a radical kind of monastic inner hospitality as we welcome in all of the strangeness that we feel in journeying to foreign places within us, exploring new dreams and possibilities. St. Benedict described hospitality as welcoming the stranger at the door as the face of Christ. The most strange, uncomfortable, unfamiliar, is the very place where we encounter God. On pilgrimage, we meet not just strangers in the outer world, but strangeness in ourselves. Navigating new worlds, learning new customs, and deepening into a foreign language are all ways of extending welcome to the stranger we meet within.

A profound kind of humility is also demanded of us. We recognize that *we* don't know what will happen on our journey. We don't understand how we will be changed by this experience. We will surely stumble and fall. When you're walking a path without a map, it is impossible to plan ahead.

Simplicity calls to us. We are invited to let go and release. This means we get to decide what we no longer want to carry with us. When we let these things go, we may feel our burdens lightened. We will focus on this invitation more deeply in the next chapter.

What will ground us is a commitment to return to the center even as we travel life's edges. We must find spaces for silence and solitude so we can listen. The monk in the world knows that holy pauses are essential for discovering the meaning of our experiences. There is no map. We can only drop deep into our hearts to guide us through our next steps.

Nature is a wise teacher. It calls us to explore what it means to live a wild life. A wild life is one that is not domesticated into boxes of safety. It is a risky way of being because in the wild there is always an encounter with fierce forces.

The alternative is to suffocate over time on dreams that dissolve by never allowing the opening of our souls. Monks are not concerned with maintaining the status quo. The first monks went out into the untamed desert looking for the edges of life. They believed that such places could be fertile and rich. When we live with the same wild heart, we remember that God can see beyond every horizon. All we need to do is trust God to lead us to more edges.

Reflection by John Valters Paintner

THE STORY OF ADAM AND EVE LEAVING THE GARDEN (GN 3:14–24)

The authors of the Hebrew scriptures believe in a good and loving Creator who made all of creation good. This foundational belief, standing in direct contrast to the prevailing beliefs of the pagan religions of their day, is sorely tested by the Babylonian exile.

Not only do the Chosen People lose the kingdom and the Temple (promised to David and Solomon) but the very Promised Land (first promised to Abraham and Sarah). Those not killed in the Babylonian invasion are either scattered across their conqueror's empire or left behind in squalor. Such a situation would test anyone's faith in a good and loving God.

The two contradictory but complementary creation stories at the start of the book of Genesis are written with the purpose of answering the great questions of suffering and evil in the world.

The first chapter of Genesis begins with a description of how God created order and abundance out of the chaotic void. For six days, God speaks into creation a world filled with every good thing. At the culmination of God's work, man and woman are created in the divine image, and it is all very good. The main actor is a divine character who is pragmatic and caring. Everything is done in an orderly fashion in preparation for the culmination of God's work: humanity.

Beginning with the second chapter of Genesis, we are told a slightly different story. A good and loving God is still the main protagonist but is now joined by a few more characters. First, the man (Adam) is created and placed in the Garden of Eden which God builds up for him. God had filled it with other animals, all of whom prove to be unsatisfying companions. This prompts God to create the woman (Eve). The man and woman have everything they need and very little in the way of restrictions.

The man and woman are tempted into disobeying God's command. They eat the forbidden fruit. When God confronts them, the woman blames the serpent. The man goes one step further when he blames God for placing the woman in the Garden with him. The fact of the matter was that they both had the same choice: trust God or trust the serpent.

The man and the woman chose poorly. They are punished with pain, suffering, and death. Worst of all, they are no longer allowed to remain in the perfect home that God created for them. They are cast out and barred from returning.

REFLECTION ON ADAM AND EVE LEAVING THE GARDEN OF EDEN

The story of Adam and Eve is an allegory of the Jewish exile from the Holy Land. Their pilgrimage is not of their choosing, but it is a result of their decisions.

When I think of a pilgrimage, I usually imagine one or more people making a deliberate, conscious decision to go on a long journey to a holy place for some specific quest (healing, penance, enlightenment, revelation). I don't often think of someone being forced out of a place to go on an undetermined journey in order to achieve a yet-to-be-named objective. They are more refugee than pilgrim, at least at the start. However, this is where Adam and Eve, and later the exiled Jews, find themselves.

Pilgrimage, in this sense, can mean the life journeys we take in response to unwelcomed circumstances. Perhaps the expulsion from the Garden is not a pilgrimage. It's about the long sense of exile in life and the long journey home. Any time life ousts us from our places of security, we are called upon to bring ourselves fully present to our experience. We honor that even unbidden journeys can take us to places where we encounter God more closely. This is the heart of the pilgrimage experience.

Adam and Eve do have one advantage, though. Our first parents possess no preconceived ideas about what a "successful" pilgrimage will be. They truly do not know what to expect, so they just take one step at a time. Without the distraction of a self-imposed, preordained destination, necessary detours are easier to see.

Their biggest hurdle, though, is heeding the call. They can't help but hear it (an angel with a flaming sword in hand is hard to miss). But hearing and accepting are two different things.

Elijah tried running away when things got too difficult. God sent him back into the fray. Jonah tried to run away when he heard his call to journey to Nineveh. A large fish deposited him exactly where he didn't want to go. Jeremiah begged God to let him quit. The words burned within him and he had to go on. Even Mary momentarily questions if she is the right one to bear the Messiah. She says yes more quickly than most, but that's what made her worthy of her journey.

I once thought I'd be a high school religion teacher until I retired. But the Thursday in February of 2012 when I was informed of the new, nation-wide curriculum being implemented by the US bishops, I went home very upset.

There had been some talk that the bishops planned on making some changes, but no one possessed any hard facts. Earlier in the week, my principal hinted at what was to come at the religion department meeting that Thursday. At the meeting, the chair of the department was a bit upset that his big surprise had been spoiled. What spoiled it for me was not just that I disagreed with the new curriculum on education and theological grounds, but that I had been given no input into the new curriculum. Moreover, the chair had already picked out the new textbooks after several meetings with administrators at the chancery. I had no say in what was happening and everyone just assumed I would go along with it.

It reminded me of a computer error message that pops up on the screen telling you of an impending computer crash and the only option is to click the button marked "OK." It's not "OK"! One does have to accept it before one can continue forward, even if one has to back-track a little first.

When I came home from that staff meeting, Christine knew right away that a great life journey was about to begin. The previous year, our daydreaming turned to actually making plans to live abroad for six months to a year. Suddenly, all the prep-work that had gone into a sabbatical year was now the groundwork for perhaps a lifelong pilgrimage.

It took me the better part of a month to come to terms with this life-changing decision and click that "OK" button on our call to pilgrimage.

INVITATION TO *LECTIO*: ADAM AND EVE LEAVE THE GARDEN OF EDEN (GN 3:23–24)

Each chapter you will be invited to pray with a different text from scripture drawn from the story we explore. Below is a set of guidelines for the practice of lectio divina. Bring this contemplative way of reading scripture to the ancient words below and see what shimmers forth for you:

> The LORD God therefore banished him from the Garden of Eden, to till the ground from which he had been taken. He expelled the man, stationing the cherubim and the fiery revolving sword east of the Garden of Eden, to guard the way to the tree of life.

First Movement—Lectio: Settling and Shimmering

Begin by finding a comfortable position where you can remain alert and yet also relax your body. Bring your attention to your breath and allow a few moments to become centered. If you find yourself distracted at any time, gently return to the rhythm of your breath as an anchor for your awareness. Allow yourself to settle into this moment and become fully present.

Read your selected scripture passage or other sacred text once or twice through slowly and listen for a word or phrase that feels significant right now, is capturing your attention even if you don't know why. Gently repeat this word to yourself in the silence.

Second Movement—Meditatio: Savoring and Stirring

Read the text again and then allow the word or phrase which caught your attention in the first movement to spark your imagination. Savor the word or phrase with all of your senses, notice what smells, sounds, tastes, sights, and feelings are evoked. Then listen for what images, feelings, and memories are stirring, welcoming them in, and then savoring and resting into this experience.

Third Movement—Oratio: Summoning and Serving

Read the text a third time and then listen for an invitation rising up from your experience of prayer so far. Considering the word or phrase and what it has evoked for you in memory, image, or feeling, what is the invitation? This invitation may be a summons toward a new awareness or action.

Fourth Movement—Contemplatio: Slowing and Stilling

Move into a time for simply resting in God and allowing your heart to fill with gratitude for God's presence in this time of prayer. Slow your thoughts even further and sink into the experience of stillness. Rest in the presence of God and allow yourself to simply be. Rest here for several minutes. Return to your breath if you find yourself distracted.

Closing

Gently connect with your breath again and slowly bring your awareness back to the room, moving from inner experience to outer experience. Give yourself some time of transition between these moments of contemplative depth and your everyday life. Consider taking a few minutes to journal about what you experienced in your prayer.

WRITING EXPLORATION THROUGH MIDRASH

Midrash is an ancient practice of the Jewish tradition. Rabbis wrote Midrash to help explain problems they encountered in the biblical texts such as inconsistencies or missing voices. These stories form an important part of the Jewish sacred literature.

In Judaism, scripture is sometimes described as black fire on white fire. Black fire is the words on the page. Midrash illuminates the white fire, the spaces between the words that are written. Through Midrash we explore the gaps in the story, the missing voices, the silences, the wondering that is sparked.

Hundreds of years later, St. Ignatius of Loyola, a Spanish mystic and founder of the Jesuit order of priests, offered a way of praying the scriptures through the imagination that had foundations in Midrash. In what is often referred to as Ignatian prayer of the imagination, we are invited into the cracks and spaces of the story to see what is revealed to us.

Ignatius believed that our imagination, senses, and feelings were holy portals into understanding the sacred. He invites us to read a text prayerfully. We are to imagine stepping into the story ourselves, seeing, hearing, tasting, smelling, and feeling what it is like to be in the scene. He suggests we have conversations with the characters to see what they might say to us in what is known as a *colloquy*. This prayer is about entering ourselves within the story and seeing what we encounter. These words of the sacred texts are meant to be alive, and because they are archetypal, they can speak to human experience across time.

Both of these practices, Midrash and Ignatian prayer, embrace the profound significance biblical stories can have for us personally when we allow ourselves to not just read at a distance. They call us to enter the texts in their own realities. Scripture was never meant to be heard just from a lectern in church. The biblical stories call us to dive in and see what we discover. There is acknowledgement of the truth that can arise in our imaginative engagement with sacred texts.

While the Jewish tradition of Midrash originated with the early Rabbis, in more recent years, the feminist movement has brought this practice alive again. Women started to search for the voices of women in the biblical narratives. This led to a whole new genre of contemporary women's Midrash that laid claim to these voices in a playful but beautiful way.

I invite you to play with this form as a possibility for creative exploration and engagement with the sacred stories we focus on in each chapter.

For this first chapter, we look at the story of Adam and Eve being banished from the Garden of Eden. This was our passage for prayer with lectio divina (Gn 3:23–24):

> The LORD God therefore banished him from the Garden of Eden, to till the ground from which he had been taken. He expelled the man, stationing the cherubim and the fiery revolving sword east of the Garden of Eden, to guard the way to the tree of life.

You can stay with this portion of the story or look in a Bible for the wider context.

Begin much in the way you would for a practice of lectio divina. Center yourself with some deep breaths, move your attention inward, begin settling into stillness.

Read the text through slowly. Imagine that you are experiencing the story right now; it is not some distant mythical account but a story meant to become alive for you.

Let yourself enter the scene with all of your senses engaged. What do you see, taste, smell, hear, and feel? Allow some time for each of these to reveal themselves.

Let yourself enter into each of the characters in the story. Imagine you are Eve reaching for the apple on the tree. What are you thinking and feeling? Imagine that you are Adam, discovering that you have been banished from this place of Paradise. Imagine that you are God experiencing the betrayal. Enter into the voice of the tree, the angel, the snake, whichever opening seems to invite you to step inside.

The important thing in this practice is not to let yourself get caught up in theological interpretation. For a moment, set aside the doctrine of original sin and the notion of Eve being blamed for the Fall. Let yourself meet the story as if for the first time and have an encounter with it. Enter into it and see what you discover from this new vantage point.

Have a conversation with Adam and Eve about their experience and longing. How do they feel about leaving the Garden? What are their hopes and fears? Do they have any wisdom for you as you begin your own great journey? Maybe you have a conversation with them about what it was like for them to first meet one another and discover each other. What are the questions that arise for you from the text? These are all just suggestions.

To write Midrash, or to pray with the imagination and enter the story, doesn't require special skill. When we engage creative expression as a process, we let go of the fear of what the end product will look like, and let ourselves yield to what the process reveals to us. Be attentive to your own experience as you move through—where do you encounter ease and where is the resistance? Just notice these with compassion and curiosity.

The most important part of this process is to pay attention to the moment in the story which stirs the most curiosity or energy for you. It might be the place of your greatest resistance, the place in the story that feels the most difficult. Stay with that energy. Where do the questions emerge?

Feel free to write in prose or poetry form. However the words emerge is perfect.

This kind of writing is a process of diving deep within and seeing what you discover. Let the process itself surprise you and take you places you didn't expect. Hold your own desire for pilgrimage and to follow your call. Use this process to explore and seek wisdom.

Sometimes writing with a limited amount of time can be helpful. Consider setting a timer for ten or fifteen minutes, reading the passage, and then seeing where your imagination takes you without trying to force things in a particular direction. Time limits can be very helpful in bypassing our analytical minds that want to spend hours finding the perfect story and writing it in the perfect form. This process is not about perfection or product but discovery and encounter. When we write in a limited time frame it can help us drop down below the inner critic and censor just long enough to access something from the heart.

Then write. It might be the thoughts and desires of a single character's experience in the moment. It might be a journey of remembering or anticipation. Often dialogue, either between you and a character or between the characters themselves, can be a place for rich exploration. Perhaps your story is just a description of the sensual richness of this place as you have encountered it in your imagination.

You aren't writing with a particular goal in mind but writing as pilgrimage, which means as a journey of discovery itself.

MIDRASH EXPLORATIONS

As the gates to the garden slammed firmly shut behind us, the tears overwhelmed me. He didn't say anything and there was a stony silence between us. I knew there would be no going back, and that somehow we would have to find a way of dealing with what had happened to us. Although it was nigh impossible to imagine, maybe we would find a new tree of life—or perhaps we would have to plant one for ourselves.

—Helen Jelfs

i stand here in the midst of a garden
raising my gnarled branches to heaven
enjoying the sun's warmth on my leaves

and the gentleness of the breezes

i listen to the bird songs and laughter
which comes from the man and woman
my fruit is so beautiful and fragrant
that i feel grateful to be bearing it

suddenly a chill rushes from my roots
to my topmost branches
a small very cold creature crawls
up my trunk and poises for attack

the woman stops and listens to him
in her innocence she believes the lie
my inmost sap stops running as she plucks
the fruit and eats sharing with the man

i hear the lord call adam and eve
and see their fear for the first time
they leave in tears as the gate closes
and the cunning snake slithers away

i stand here in the garden alone and sad

—Rosemary Hall

VISIO DIVINA: SEEING WITH EYES OF THE HEART

Visio divina (sacred seeing) is a way of seeing the world with the eyes
of the heart, which is the place of openness, rather than with the mind,
which is often the place of planning. It is an adaptation of the ancient
practice of lectio divina (sacred reading).

For each chapter you are invited, as part of your pilgrimage, to go
on a contemplative walk and receive images along the way which might
offer insight or wisdom for the theme we are exploring.

During a contemplative walk, your sole focus is on being present
to each moment's invitation as it unfolds, rather than setting out with
a particular goal. There is nowhere to "get to." You begin by breathing

deeply and centering yourself, bringing your awareness down to your heart center.

Go out in the world for a walk. It could be just down your block or in a nearby park. Bring a camera—a simple camera on your phone is fine. As you walk stay present to the world as a sacred text, much like you would in lectio divina with the scriptures. Hold the chapter theme gently in your imagination. Below is a suggested process to move through.

Settling and Shimmering

Breathe deeply. Move your awareness down to your heart center. Settle into this moment. Release any thoughts or expectations. See if you can keep a soft gaze which is diffuse and open, as opposed to a hard stare as if you are looking for something.

As you begin walking, pay attention to things around you that shimmer, which means something that calls for your attention, invites you to spend some time with it. It might be a natural object like a tree or branch, it might be a sign in a shop window that catches your attention, or the way light is flooding the street. Stay open to all possibilities for how the world might speak to your heart.

Savoring and Stirring

Stay with what shimmers and allow it to unfold in your heart, savoring your experience.

Make space within for images, feelings, and memories to stir. How does your body respond? What are you noticing happening inside in response to this experience?

Summoning and Serving

Slowly shift your awareness to a sense of invitation or summoning which rises up from your prayer. How does the prayer stirring in you meet you in this particular moment of your life? How might you be called into a new awareness or kind of service through this experience?

You might explore with your camera how gazing at this shimmering moment through the lens supports you in seeing it more deeply. The practice of contemplative photography is to "receive images as gifts" rather than to "take photos." If you notice yourself grasping, put the camera down. But if the lens is helping you to see this moment from different perspectives, then the camera can be a great gift.

Slowing and Stilling

Once your walk feels complete, you must re-enter the world by returning home to a place of quiet. Release all of the words, images, and ideas. Allow yourself some time for silence and stillness. Breathe gratitude in and out. Simply notice your experience.

PHOTOGraPHIC PILGrimage

One of the things I love about photography is its accessibility. Many of us have cameras on our phones which we carry around all the time. You do not need fancy equipment for this practice. This is a practice of learning to receive gifts rather than take photos. You go out in the world with open palms and see what you discover.

This first chapter's theme is on call and response. As you journey out into the world hold this image gently in your imagination. Notice if there are images around you which shimmer forth. Receive them with gratitude, noticing when you start to grasp at taking photos rather than simply letting the images arrive to you as gifts.

When you return home, spend some time softly gazing on the photos you received in this journey. See if they have anything to say to you about your own calling to pilgrimage. Spend some time journaling with the images. Sometimes it can be helpful to dialogue with them, asking what wisdom they have to offer to you.

CLOSInG BLeSSInG

You have been really listening for the call in your life and how you might respond with a yes, even if that call arose out of events you wish didn't happen. Pilgrimage invites us to allow all of life to become an intentional journey, even in the midst of loss and grief. It is a call to find ourselves and God in new ways.

I offer you this poem about following the call that beats in our blood, arising from a place we don't understand, but must follow. Bless you as you say yes, as you swim against the currents, as you journey in the direction you must go.

Following an Ancient Call

What if we could listen
like the great salmon
who goes about its ordinary life
when suddenly something shifts.

It does not come as a thunderous
revelation, but a quiet knowing
you have been preparing all
your life to trust.

The path lived until now no longer
satisfies but the path ahead
seems thousands of miles
long, and your womb is heavy.

There is no refusing this ancient call,
and to know ourselves as not alone,
but part of generations before us who,
like the salmon, share in this inheritance.

You now hear only the rush of energy
that comes with starting the long
return home and the pull in the
blood which cannot be ignored.

I like to imagine the salmon
swimming across the ocean
(as if that weren't daunting enough)
and after that endless voyage

it must face the mouth of the mighty river.
Does she hesitate, even for a moment?
Does he want to turn back to less turbulent waters?
But there is something ripening in their bellies.

Perhaps your list of pressing tasks is still long.
Leave it there fluttering in the breeze,
uncrossed, undone, unfinished,
to do the only thing you can do

which is to swim,
to be carried by the waves and tide
and to know when to let the current carry you
and when to fight it with all your strength,

and to know even this *yes* will
demand more than you were willing
to give: your life for the new birth,
what you think you know for

the ancient call home.

Chapter 2

THE PRACTICE OF PACKING LIGHTLY

*When we feel more secure, powerful, confident, and self-suf-
ficient, we are nothing. We are most abjectly not. But when
we're stripped naked by desert despair, helplessly and hopeless-
ly decreated by all of our facades and deceptions, we are most
real, most substantial. We are. Our being is in proportion to
the destitution forced on us by the wilderness.*

—**Kerry Walters**, *Soul Wilderness*

SELLING EVERYTHING

When John and I made the decision to move overseas, we faced major
decisions about what do about our things. We lived in Seattle for nine
years, and no matter how much we tried to be mindful about simplicity,
we accumulated *lots* of things. Our two bedroom apartment with a few
closets seemed to contain secret pockets of stuff.

We loved our cozy home, but we needed to decide whether to sell
or rent. At that point, we weren't sure how long we would be away, but
we couldn't shake the sense we might be going on a long-term journey.
If that was the case, we didn't want to carry the burden of dealing with
tenants. We chose total freedom, which seemed like the best direction
for discernment.

Thankfully, we hit the real estate market during a "seller's market."
The house sold in three days at full price, which seemed to be a confir-
mation of our desire to simplify.

We received enough from the house sale to pay off all but two hundred dollars of our graduate student loans. Debt can be a burden on a journey, and we didn't want to carry it with us.

We sold some of our furniture, many of our books, and gave the rest away. We decided to keep one storage unit, the smallest available size, to hold two pieces of furniture from my grandparents and some bins of family photos. A friend wanted to buy a good quality used car and so our ten-year-old, well-cared-for vehicle went to a good home.

As I look back on this time two years later, I remember bouncing from sheer panic to self-doubt and finally arriving at feeling free. We entered a different season in our life at just the right time.

Many friends tell me they could never do what we did. I remind them we had little choice. The call to pilgrimage came like a whirlwind and we could not ignore it. Thankfully, the call to simplicity as a lifelong practice helped us. I tell my friends that following in our footsteps doesn't require they sell everything. It's not about proving how little you need to go on a journey. Rather, it's about following the call to "go."

packing your bags for the journey

One of the great gifts of travel is how it makes me focus on the things I choose to carry with me. Heavy baggage becomes a burden. The pilgrim doesn't want to be weighed down with things that are unnecessary for the journey. She seeks to carry only what is essential. This is, of course, a metaphor for life. Consider the things in your life and perhaps make a commitment to give away something every week for the next season. Think about what you can give to a local charity or to the library. Ask yourself what requires too much energy to sustain anymore.

Broaden your vision for what you carry. Imagine what kinds of attitudes, beliefs, expectations, and stories you tell about yourself that don't need to go with you. As the storyteller Michael Meade once said, "a false sense of security is the only kind there is." We are often disappointed when we make choices out of the idea of how things should be in our lives. This point of view is often influenced by the logic of the world. However, the wisdom of calling usually flies in the face of that logic.

As part of your pilgrimage, what are the things you want to carry with you and what are the things (both tangible and intangible) you can lay down for this season ahead?

Pilgrimage demands preparation. There is much letting go that needs to happen. Packing bags means we need to discern what to carry with us and what to leave behind. This is one of the great gifts of pilgrimage; an invitation to discern what is essential.

What keeps you from the great adventure life is calling you to? What are the logical or practical explanations that get in your way? What needs to be released to travel more lightly?

THE MONASTIC PRACTICE OF SIMPLICITY

It was said of Abba Paul that he spent the whole of Lent eating only one measure of lentils, drinking one small jug of water, and working on one single basket, weaving it and unweaving it, living alone until the feast.

—**Paul the Simple,** *The Sayings of the Desert Fathers*

The desert monks focused on asceticism as a way to let go of attachments and find pleasure in that which is really important. Asceticism, at its heart center, is about letting go of everything that keeps us from God and moving us along a journey toward authentic freedom. Desert ascetics kept their possessions to a minimum and practiced fasting as a way of attending to the body. If a monk fasted to the point of harming the body, he would be disciplined. Yet, even then, certain monks ended up starving themselves to death.

The desert monks lived simple lives in a stone hut, slept on a reed mat with a sheep-skin for warmth, a lamp to see by, and a container for water. Food and sleep were reduced to the very minimum needed to sustain oneself. Anything that caused a distraction to focusing on God got cut out. They kept silence so they could hear God more clearly and fasted from the distraction of noise. The monks committed to supporting themselves through the work of their own hands.

Fasting isn't just for its own sake. When we fast from food, we are called to become keenly aware of our relationship to food and to pay attention to our own hungers. The monks knew that fasting was an invitation to see what happens when we don't have our normal, everyday securities. They considered one meal for the day sufficient.

Fasting is really an invitation to authentic freedom. It is meant to free us from things that might weigh us down or restrict us. What kind of things? It could be anything from material possessions to personal beliefs. Whatever might hinder us in our search for God's face.

We might consider, as a part of this pilgrimage, fasting from ideas that keep us from truly living or thoughts that don't nourish us in spirit. We hold onto ideas about ourselves that keep us limited from everything we can be in our lives.

Words bombard us from every angle either through old stories, a turned up radio, or a television broadcasting the words of others. We use them to hide what is happening to us on the inside and that helps us lose touch with ourselves.

I adore books. They are essential to my work and writing, and when we lived in Seattle, my many bookcases full of great wisdom seemed easy to justify. So, I learned to check in with myself: Do I really need this book? Am I avoiding embracing my own wisdom by relying on the words of others? This is a delicate balance because I believe that books open up new worlds and the ideas of others do help me grow.

In our big move, we ended up selling most of our books and that horrified many of my friends. Truth be told, it horrified me too. I didn't want to give them up. This reluctance, however, clued me into something about books I never considered.

Books can have a shadow side. They might lead us to believe that we need more information so we can feel complete. Sometimes we buy more books as a surrogate for living because we believe those books contain life. We need to examine whether we're being fully present to ourselves and understanding our hunger for knowledge.

The invitation from the desert elders here is to practice simplicity first. When we find this simplicity, they believed, we find true life. This will mean different things for each of us, but we all know when something makes us alive. The interesting part comes when we realize we also have ways of avoiding the things that give us life.

The root of the word "monk" is *monos*, which means one or single. It isn't so much about marital status as it is about the condition of one's heart. When I try to live as a monk, I commit to living my life with as much integrity as possible. "Integrity" has the same root as the words "integral" and "integrated": *integritatem* means wholeness and soundness. When I act with integrity, it means I'm always moving toward wholeness and oneness. I seek to avoid being divided. In doing so, I find myself back to the root of *monos*. The desert monks call us to this singleness of heart and to live from this commitment.

As you pack your bags for this journey, you might ask yourself a series of questions. What items are necessary? What function (if any) do they serve? What would happen if you left them behind? Imagine carrying these items with you in a suitcase from place to place as you travel. Is it worth the weight?

Anytime we have a desert experience in our lives, something is stripped away. It may be loss of possessions, loss of identity, or loss of a loved one. We are meant to feel grief over these events and to fully experience the pain that comes in these moments. This stripping away forces us to return to the essence of things. We are thrust into the arms of what is most sacred to us.

We must practice this kind of letting go each day. Learn to apply it to possessions as you seek to consume less. Give more to those in need. Let go of your compulsive thoughts and release expectations. All of these prepare us for the bigger moments of letting go.

LETTING GO OF THINGS

Consider what are the things in your life you could do without. If there are things in your home that are never used, might they go to a good home? There is such freedom in clearing out space.

LETTING GO OF COMMITMENTS

Consider also the commitments of time you make that no longer enliven you. Perhaps you are part of a committee and it is time to let someone else take on the responsibilities. Look through your calendar and see if there are things that are not essential. What would free up more space so that you can breathe deeply and sit in stillness?

LETTING GO OF RELATIONSHIPS

This invitation is trickier and requires more consideration. Are there people in your life who drain you of energy? Maybe you discover your doctor or dentist isn't a good fit for you anymore, so you try seeking out someone new. Perhaps there is someone in your life you get together with purely out of obligation. What about an old friend who complains and criticizes all the time? Consider how you might free yourself a bit from this sense of responsibility and allow yourself more space for what is essential.

LETTING GO OF BELIEFS AND IDEAS

What are the beliefs and expectations you hold about the world that could be released? Perhaps it is a sense of cynicism about people's motivations or a sense of your own limitations based on old wounds. This is perhaps the most challenging of the calls because these beliefs and thought patterns are more subtle, more deeply ingrained. But the other layers of letting go eventually bring you to deeper awareness of how much baggage you are still carrying in other ways.

CONSIDERING WHAT TO CARRY WITH YOU

One traditional symbol for the pilgrim's journey is the scallop shell. The grooves on the shell represent the different journeys we take as pilgrims. Just as all the separate grooves meet at the end of the shell, so do all of our paths meet in the same place. The journey of a pilgrimage is about returning home with a new awareness of what home really means.

Many ancient cultures used shells for drinking cups or makeshift bowls. They became very practical tools of the home that could be carried on long journeys. So consider if you might be able to find a scallop shell to keep as a symbol for this time. Let it remind you not only of the journey but also of your destination.

Another symbol pilgrims carried with them is the pilgrim's staff, a walking stick offering support for the journey. You might already have a walking stick you could set beside your prayer chair. If not, take a walk in the woods by yourself to find one.

I once found the perfect stick. As a way to make it my own, I decorated it with tissue paper and paint. Find your own stick and make it your own. Maybe you prefer a more natural look made by attaching feathers or even your scallop shell.

You might have a special candle you light for this season each time you sit down to reflect or create. Your journal might be a symbol of your own unfolding story.

Imagine yourself joining in the company of Abraham and Sarah and being called far away from what is familiar. Carry with you only what is necessary for your soul's nourishment.

creating a guidebook for the journey

I invite you to consider what would feed you in the coming weeks—not through food or drink but a nourishment of the soul—through poetry, sacred texts, music, art, and film. These can enrich our lives by offering us symbols for how to walk the path ahead of us.

In medieval times, pilgrims would set all their affairs in order, including any debts. They would wear a pilgrim robe and carry a walking stick. They would make a vow to their priest to complete the journey. They would then go in search of the trail of scallop shells left by other pilgrims.

They would also carry a small book called a *vade mecum*, which in Latin means "go with me". This book contained prayers, wisdom, and maps for the journey. Very often, the pilgrims would create symbols on the pages to remind them of their way. You are invited to create your own guidebook or *vade mecum* for this pilgrimage. Gather poems, prayers, blessings, art, photos, dream images, and anything else that comes to mind as soul encouragement for the journey. There may be a poem or line from a book that strikes you. It may just be one or two things. Gather the things together that speak to your heart.

Consider adding them to your journal. This will be a container, a holding space for the words and images which come your way. It is an

ongoing process, but one which calls you to pay attention to the way
symbols are emerging in the world around you. It is a practice of honoring that which most deeply nurtures your own soul longings.

What are the prayers which sustain you?

journey prayers and blessings

Journeying god,
pitch your tent with mine
so that I may not become deterred
by hardship, strangeness, doubt.
Show me the movement I must make
toward a wealth not dependent on possessions,
toward a wisdom not based on books,
toward a strength not bolstered by might,
toward a god not confined to heaven.
Help me to find myself as I walk in other's shoes.

—**Prayer song from Ghana**, traditional

Imagine the season ahead offering a blessing for each time you leave
home, no matter the errand or distance. Remember God's holy presence
in all of life and especially the times of transition.

Write your own prayer of blessing for the many journeys of your
life—both outer and inner.

You might take inspiration from the journey blessings above. What
words arise as you ponder the ways you want to remember the sacred
always with you through all of life's footsteps?

Reflection by John Valters Paintner

THE STORY OF ABRAM AND SARAI CALLED TO LEAVE HOME (GN 12:1–9)

Chapter twelve marks a dramatic change in the book of Genesis. The
Bible turns away from stories about the creation of the world (and the

origins of suffering) to stories about the creation of a people and a nation. It becomes a very personal story.

Following the infamous tales of Cain and Abel (where the sinful ways of Adam and Eve continue in their children), Noah and the Great Flood (where the general sinfulness of humanity causes God to hit the "reset" button on creation), and the Tower of Babel (where humans are so blinded by their sinfulness that they think they can become equals to God), a short genealogy brings us to Abraham and Sarah . . . or as we first meet them, Abram and Sarai (but more of that later).

The story begins with Abram's father, Terah, who takes his family out of their native Ur (in present-day Iraq). Terah plans to travel all the way to Canaan but settles only a short distance away in Haran. After Terah's death, Abram receives the Lord's call to go to Canaan. Abram is to leave behind the land where he was born.

The Lord calls him to travel to an unknown and distant land. Abram takes with him his wife (Sarai) and his nephew (Lot), along with his possessions (including a small herd and a few servants). In modern terms, Abram doesn't exactly pack lightly, but for a nomad, Abram doesn't have much with him when he leaves.

The greater significance is not what they bring with them but what they leave behind. It is not going to an alien landscape which was the greatest sacrifice for Abram and Sarai. Rather, they would never see their family and clan (except one nephew) again. In their tribal society, the meaning of their lives was bound in the concept of one's family. If you left that behind, it was like a death in a very real sense. Abram and Sarai begin their great pilgrimage with very little support for their journey.

REFLECTION ON ABRAM AND SARAI CALLED TO LEAVE HOME

In the early stages of planning our move to Europe, our idea was to go for a year's sabbatical. Christine and I made tentative plans for my niece (and perhaps nephew) to house and dog sit for us while we were away. We thought we'd travel light and keep most of our belongings safely at home awaiting our return. However, when the sabbatical year became an open-ended, one-way journey, we received a radical new perspective on possessions.

Nothing makes you reevaluate how much you want to have something quite like the thought of having to move it from Point A to Point B. It's no longer just about desire and ascetics. It's not even about sentimentality. Size and weight take on very practical implications when moving objects across oceans.

We had molded our cozy little condo in Seattle the way we wanted it when the call to pilgrimage came. The improvements we made helped during the selling process but made it even more difficult to let go.

Clothes were fairly easy to pare down. It's easy to get rid of things that just sit in closets and drawers. The books, on the other hand, would have been impossible if not for the help of an old college friend of Christine's who owned a used bookstore.

We walked through the familiar haunts of our Seattle neighborhood. As we did, I recognized our weekly routine as we passed by our favorite dining spots and the farmer's market. I thought about our friends in each of these places. On our pilgrimage, we would make new routines and new friends. The thought of these possibilities was exciting and overwhelming.

Soon, we faced the awful truth that taking a pit bull mix into Europe wasn't going to happen. We would need to give her to a new family. Needless to say, giving her away for our journey was heart wrenching.

Winter had always been a country dog. She'd grown accustomed to living in the city, but she really needed large open spaces. Her free spirit needed fields, mud puddles, and the company of other dogs.

I'd like to think Winter misses us, but her new home out in the country has allowed her to be her true self. Sometimes letting go is the best thing to do, even when it is the hardest.

While Christine and I don't come from large families, leaving them would turn out to be the hardest part. We are blessed to live in an era where technology allows us to keep in close contact with family and friends far away. We can talk to them through the miracle of the Internet or jump on a plane to make a journey that used to take months. Abram and Sarai never had those luxuries. Their journey was one-way. There was no going back for them and very little opportunity for communication with family "back home."

Yet the journey did not change Abram and Sarai right away. Just as they crawled along the landscape of Mesopotamia, the changes in their souls occurred over time. Simply going on their great pilgrimage was not enough. They had things to do and learn before they were transformed into their new identities. They went through numerous trials by fire and changes in landscape before the Lord gave them new identities by giving them new names. However, they could not have taken on their new person if they had not been willing to let go of their old selves.

This is the difference between being a tourist and a pilgrim. A tourist has new experiences, but remains the same person. A pilgrim experiences new places and is transformed by them. We can only be freed by what lies ahead if we leave behind our baggage.

INVITATION TO *LECTIO*: ABRAM AND SARAI CALLED TO LEAVE HOME (GN 12:1–2)

The LORD said to Abram: Go forth from your land, your relatives, and from your father's house to a land that I will show you. I will make of you a great nation, and I will bless you; I will make your name great, so that you will be a blessing.

WRITING EXPLORATION THROUGH MIDRASH

We introduced you to the practice of writing Midrash in the previous chapter and invite you into the practice again. Our scripture story is of Abraham and Sarah being called to go forth to a new land. It is the call of pilgrimage, and they must leave behind everything that is familiar, land and relatives, and carry forth only what is needed.

Begin by finding a quiet space and settle into the rhythm of your breath. Drop your awareness out of your thinking mind. Open up yourself to the intuitive and receiving space of your heart. Imagine yourself stepping into the scripture text. See the world around you, this place where Abraham and Sarah have lived most of their lives. Get in touch with all that is familiar and comforting for them. Open yourself through all of your senses to the experience of this place.

Hear the call from God; imagine how it comes to them, whether through a voice in the silence or a clanging announcement. Imagine Abraham and Sarah's reaction. What do they talk about with one another? What are their fears? What are the places of resistance? What kind of grief does this bring up for them?

Enter into conversation with each of them. Bring your own desire to be on a great pilgrimage and seek their wisdom. What words do they have to offer to you?

Let yourself write for a limited amount of time, bypassing the inner critic, and see what story arises.

MIDraSH EXPLOraTIONS

Abraham and Sarah felt comfortable. More than comfortable at home. Home was defined by fig trees and date wine and the ripple in the linen curtains that the breeze at dusk made, sweeping in the darkness of night. This wasn't something to leave. And yet, the calling came, perhaps in the middle of the night, perhaps at the well when the urge to draw water from the earth wasn't enough. The call came and despite all efforts to quell it, they had to listen. But how to explain this to the Others? Moreso, how to explain this to themselves? At least they were two, and the call was shared, and ultimately, what they decided was that the call reached back through generations and forward into the distant future and that they were just two on a moving thread through history, they were just two, and also many.

—**Sarah Shellow**

It is three o'clock in the morning and I cannot sleep. I wanted to wake Sarai and hold her in my arms. I am having second thoughts. She looked so peaceful and she worked so hard to get ready for this journey, I didn't want to burden her. I wish I could sleep like she does. I came out of the tent to take some air, to just look at the stars. I needed to be alone. The stars are so clear and bright, and I cannot count them all. I can't count the number of times I have been awake at night wondering what I am doing here, praying to You for help, looking for a sign that what I am doing matters to You, to the people I love who are looking to me for help. I get out of my bed and sit alone in the dark, my thoughts swirling in my head, and I wait in the silence to hear Your Voice in my heart. Tomorrow I will leave this place where I am known and loved, where I have lived for so long. My friends think I am crazy, that I am too old for all this, that it is too risky. I am afraid that they are right. What I do know is that this life I have lived here is not enough, even though it looks like I have everything. My spirit is restless, even in my old age. I believe against all the evidence that You have something more in store for me, that there is more life calling to me, more than I can imagine, and I need You to show it to me. So I suppose that is why I am leaving everything behind me, and just setting out with only your Voice to guide me, the one I have heard all my life, Who always brings me home.

—Barbara DeCoursey Roy

CREATIVE EXPLORATION THROUGH PHOTOGRAPHY

Each chapter of this book will invite you into a visual art exploration through photography as a contemplative practice. If another visual art form, such as drawing or collage, sparks your imagination and heart even more, then please follow that intuition.

Contemplate this image of packing lightly for the journey, and then as you walk in the world, just notice images that shimmer. You don't need to look for things or try to make a logical connection in your mind between the theme and the images calling to you. This is often a form of grasping. When you notice this happening, take a deep breath, and return to this posture of receiving. Be mindful of noticing and what is happening in the moment. Don't think about what you expect to have happen.

After returning from your mini-pilgrimage, spend some time with the images which shimmered forth. Ask what wisdom they have to offer you.

When embarking on a pilgrimage it is an opportunity to consider what we might leave behind. What weight can be lifted from our shoulders? Ponder what we want to bring with us. What sacred objects or talismans might we carry along for reminders of your intention for this journey?

CLOSINg BLESSINg

This has been an invitation to strip away, and surrender, in service of making more space for what is most important. In my experience, the more I set aside the things which burden me by taking up too much space, the more I open myself to wonder. When I'm in awe, I become more grateful. I become free to see the world as enchanted.

My hope is that your heart has been opened a little bit more to the possibility of wonder as practice and posture in the world. On the pilgrim path, unencumbered by so many things, may you make many wondrous discoveries. The practice of packing lightly opens our heart to delight in the simple beauty of the world.

Invite Wonder

> What if you bowed
> before every dandelion you met
> and wrote love letters to
> squirrels and pigeons
> who crossed your path?
>
> What if scrubbing the dishes became
> an act of single reverence for the gift
> of being washed clean, and what if the
> rhythmic percussion of chopping carrots
> became the drumbeat of your dance?
>
> What if you stepped into the shower
> each morning only to be baptized anew
> and sent forth to serve the grocery bagger,
> the bank teller, and the bus driver
> through simple kindness?
>
> And what if the things that make
> your heart dizzy with delight were
> no longer stuffed into the basement
> of your being and allowed out to play
> in the lush and green fields?
> There are two ways to live in this world:

As if everything were enchanted
or nothing at all.

There is no in between, although you
keep trying to live this divided life knowing
deep down something is awry.
You have lived long enough
with this tearing apart.

Come out into the wide world
and discover there, companions and guides
at every turn, and even those who summon
curses from your heart have
a divine spark within them bright enough

to invite wonder.

Chapter 3

THE PRACTICE OF CROSSING THE THRESHOLD

At any time you can ask yourself: At which threshold am I now standing? At this time in my life, what am I leaving? Where am I about to enter? What is preventing me from crossing my next threshold? What give would enable me to do it? A threshold is not a simple boundary; it is a frontier that divides two different territories, rhythms, and atmospheres.

—John O'Donohue, *To Bless the Space Between Us*

THE THRESHOLD OF THE DESERT

In the third- to-sixth-century desert landscape of Egypt, Syria, Palestine, and Arabia, a powerful movement was happening. Christian monasticism flowered in response to a call to leave behind the world. The movement found its center in Egypt, and by 400 CE, it became the land of monks experimenting with different varieties of monasticism. Some chose to live the life of solitary hermits while others started gathering into a monastic communal life.

These spiritual seekers who came to be known as the "Desert Fathers and Mothers" withdrew from society. They believed the misuse of human relationships, power, and material possessions ran counter to their sacred sense of life.

Their journey into the desert was the crossing of a threshold towards an intentional awareness of God's presence and recognizing that worldly pleasures bring little long-term satisfaction. The aim was to experience God in each moment and activity. They did so by reducing their physical needs and committing themselves to prayer. Further, they examined themselves with brutal honesty. These monks set in motion a monastic movement that changed our world. It's amazing how their work resonates hundreds of years later.

By making the arduous journey into the desert, women rejected the patriarchal restrictions and found a life-giving alternative. In the desert, the *ammas* (mothers) were able to live with the same single focus as the *abbas* (fathers). They could achieve a growing intimacy with the divine presence in the same way as men. The rough wilds became their freedom.

These women could go as deep in their spiritual wisdom as their male counterparts. The titles of spiritual Father or Mother didn't come through a nurturing role. Instead, such honor went to those who became wise elders through a rough shaping through years in the desert.

The Desert Mothers came from a variety of backgrounds. Some came from the conventional lives of the well-educated and the wealthy. Some came from the streets where they scratched out a living through thievery or prostitution. When God called them, they left everything behind and sought a way out of their cultural constraints. The *ammas* show us that God always intended for women to be a part of introducing new patterns in the life of the church.

A Story From Amma Theodora

Theodora lived in fourth-century Egypt and not much is known about her. She found herself being a spiritual director to bishops and other men in public position. One of the few things we know about her is that she gave us a description of *acedia*, or the lack of initiative in spiritual practice.

One of the traditions of the desert came as people sought a "word." We find this term often in the stories of pilgrims who would seek out a spiritual father and mother. They'd often ask the desert monastics, "Give me a word." By "word" they meant a phrase or image they could chew on for days or even weeks. They wanted wisdom that would work on their souls.

We know that Amma Theodora had ten sayings attributed to her. That isn't to say she didn't have a lot more. Instead, they are the ten phrases that someone wrote down.

Imagine her speaking to you across 1,700 years from the harsh landscape of the Egyptian desert. Imagine this woman who had the courage to step beyond the conventions and limitations of her time. Think about how she crossed a threshold into a place that demanded radical simplicity.

However, for all its demands, it gave her the thing she longed for the most. She wanted to be one with God, free of cultural norms that would restrict or deny her the opportunity. As she grew in wisdom, even men sought her leadership and guidance until she became revered through the centuries. Amma Theodora said,

> Let us strive to enter by the narrow gate. Just as the trees, if they have not stood before the winter's storms cannot bear fruit, so it is with us; this present age is a storm and it is only through many trials and temptations that we can obtain an inheritance in the kingdom of heaven.[1]

After you have sat with the story, journal about whatever associations come up. Maybe you feel a strong resistance? Maybe you feel drawn to the images? Perhaps you don't feel anything at all. Just reflect on what your experience is, naming it.

Try not to go into analysis mode. Remember the threshold isn't about figuring things out. When you explore these thresholds, it's about resting into mystery. Learn to live in the liminal space where the old is released but the new hasn't come into being. See what response emerges for you in this space.

I love this story for many reasons, but especially because it is a call to cross a threshold. "Let us strive to enter by the narrow gate."

Amma Theodora is making reference to this passage in the Christian scriptures: "Enter through the narrow gate; for the gate is wide and the road is easy that leads to destruction, and there are many who take it. For the gate is narrow and the road is hard that leads to life, and there are few who find it" (Mt 7:13–14). This journey of crossing the threshold is about what leads to life, and yet remarkably, few choose it.

"Inheritance in the kingdom of heaven" is also a beautiful image, especially when we consider it is right here, right now, all around us. I love the word "inheritance." It means to receive from an ancestor or

as a legacy. This is the journey we are on right now. Our inheritance of
ancient stories and wisdom are knitted into our being so that the kingdom of heaven opens her gates to us. The promise of new life is ours if
we only say yes.

The Desert Mothers and Fathers valued their monastic cell as a vi-
tally important place. As with all things, they view their cells as a way to
experience stillness and as a place to quiet their inner life.

Much of the desert journey is about becoming present in our emotional life. The pilgrimage helps us see our own feelings, thoughts, and
voices that we battle. The gate is narrow because there are few who are
brave enough to enter this inner cell and stay present to the storms.

I seek to stand and stay present to my own experience. I want to
make space to feel this grief, welcome my feelings of helplessness, and
rage at injustice; I let it all in.

Gregory Mayers writes in *Listen to the Desert*:

> In times of inner turmoil and in the urgency to find a resolution to
> the confusion or an escape from it, rather than be hostage to your
> anguish, be attentive to the process as it is happening. Be attentive to
> the shame and fear, the emptiness and despondency, with which the
> ego greets the dawning wholeness. Take the middle course during
> the stormy period of transformation. Don't tamper with it. Let it
> happen. Let go.[2]

When we begin to cross the threshold, we are confronted with the
greatness of our unknowing. We are called to recognize that we do not
know what the future brings. This allows us to rest in humility rather
than theological platitudes. We may want to try and come to some resolution to obtain a feeling of control. Yet that is another way we run away
from the fierceness of the storm.

The practice is that we stay present with ourselves on this journey.
We should not abandon the call luring us forward. We should avoid going back to the comfortable. It is well for us to remember how the familiar suffocated our inner and outer lives.

Be mindful of the fact that journeys, while they often exhilarate, can
also bring feelings of fear. When we begin to entertain the possibility of

something new, we may find ourselves deluged by those critical inner voices.

PILGRIMAGE AS THRESHOLD LIVING

When we embark on an intentional journey like a pilgrimage, we are making a commitment to live in the space of threshold. Threshold is the liminal place, the place of not knowing how things will turn out. I believe it is the place of possibility.

When John and I embarked on our own life pilgrimage we did not know how things would unfold. We moved to Vienna as the first place of our heart longing. While we loved it there, we soon felt the tug towards Ireland.

We soon realized that saying yes to the first threshold of leaving home meant that we would be brought to threshold after threshold. Every one challenged us to see if we had the courage to cross. They prompted us to ask if we could live with the ambiguity or if we could trust in the mystery.

As you continue on your inner pilgrimage, what are the thresholds of your own life? Which thresholds are calling you to cross but feel difficult to face or challenging to imagine?

THRESHOLDS

A voice comes to your soul saying,
Lift your foot. Cross over.
Move into emptiness
of question and answer and question.

—Rumi, *The Glance*

The Celtic people have a wonderful term to describe the in-between moments and places. They believed that heaven and earth often came together in the "thin places." These are times when we feel that we can see through the veil and threshold is near. The thin places are a gift for us to dwell in and feel the presence of the holy through stepping out of the ordinary awareness of our days.

Thresholds, liminal space, being on the edge, living in the border-lands when we have a spirituality that is committed to exploring these rich places, it is the opposite of comfortable, safe, secure, boundaries, rigid, and unquestioned.

Thresholds require that we be vulnerable, that we acknowledge that we simply do not know what is to come. They call us to surrender to something much bigger and more meaningful, even as it calls us away from familiar patterns that are loved.

My sense is that as you continue this journey and you encounter a myriad of feelings rising up in you, it may tempt you back to sleep. You may wonder if the seemingly solid and well-worn path you have trav-eled is enough.

See if you can welcome this tender, doubting, wondering part of yourself. Give him or her room inside of you to dwell alongside your inner adventurer and risk-taker. As thoughts rise up though, again, re-lease them. Don't follow them down their trail to confusion.

You have responded to the call of pilgrimage in your life and taken a journey out into the wilderness. You will face temptation. The challenge is whether you can stay awake and present enough to notice when this is happening. What is your favorite form of self-numbing that takes your awareness away from what is happening both within and without? Can you fast from this for the season ahead to stay present to how God is moving through you?

THE PRESENCE OF ANGELS

In the Gospel of Mark, we are offered a glimpse into the pilgrimage Je-sus took out into the desert where "wild beasts" were with him (1:13). There is another element of this passage that I so often overlook: "and the angels waited on him." There might be wild beasts to encounter: the fierce ones in your own heart. But there are also powers there to help support and guide you. Remember that the threshold is full of shim-mering presence.

Much of my personal inner work is around family systems and ancestry. I believe that the wounds and blessings of my ancestors run through my blood. Their stories are my own stories. When I embark on a pilgrimage I call on their assistance. Sometimes we forget this great "cloud of witnesses" and "communion of saints" who travel alongside of us through life offering their wisdom through the veil.

Pause here for a moment. Is there an ancestor, whether genetic or spiritual, whom you could call on for help? Is there someone who took risks or someone for whom you would like to make this journey on behalf?

When I am beginning something risky, I call upon both my grandmothers. One was a teacher and the other a dancer before they got married. They gave up these passions to start a family. I offer these journeys on their behalf, knowing I am doing it for them as much as for myself. I ask for their blessings and support along the way.

inhabitants of the world's edge

The Celtic church grew on the very borders of civilization, at the outer edge of Europe and beyond much of the reach of the Roman Empire. In a seventh-century letter to Pope Boniface IV, St. Columbanus described his people as *ultimi habitatores mundi*, "inhabitants of the world's edge." They lived at the very fringes of the ancient world and embraced the perspective.

I love this image and wonder what it would mean for each of us to claim that identity. What does it mean to be an inhabitant of the world's edge? What does it mean to go out to the thresholds and wild places? What does it look like to explore holy darkness? What will it feel like when I embrace a fertile expanse of possibility beyond the safe constructs of culture that suffocate our hearts?

Many monks, when founding monasteries, created what are known as "diserts" or "dysarts," rooted in the idea of desert. David Adam in his book *Border Lands* describes them this way,

> The *disert* place of retreat was set up to discover the edge of glory, to experience the beyond that is in our midst. "Diserts" are set up not to run away from what is going on, but to experience in greater depth the reality that is about them.[3]

The *disert* is a threshold space where one can dwell between worlds. It is the container for the inner pilgrimage. Across the landscapes of Wales and in Ireland we can find over five hundred places named *disert*.

The Irish knew that the physical desert landscape could not be found in the lush terrain of their island, but the spirit of the inner desert, the cave of the heart, the cell, was found within. We are called to cultivate this interior space. We are invited to welcome in the edge that is right in our midst. When we stay present, we welcome the questions and learn not to seek the answers right away.

For this time of pilgrimage, create your own place of *disert*, a place of stillness and silence. Plunge yourself into the depths of what is most real. Let it be a place where you welcome in the wisdom of Miriam and Moses for your journey, where you remember this ancient call to pilgrimage.

In the coming days, take some time to wander out to "edge places." Bless each threshold you cross when you pass through a doorway, so that you might remember to be open to new things. Bless the threshold moments of each day as dawn arises and dusk descends. Then listen for what they have to whisper about your own threshold crossing.

Reflection by John Valters Paintner

THE STORY OF MIRIAM AT THE SEA OF REEDS (EX 12:31–42; 14:10–15:21)

It's important to note the slow progression of the ten plagues. They start off as more of a nuisance than anything else. The plagues do become increasingly serious and dangerous to plant and animal life as the stand-off between Yahweh and the Egyptian gods escalates.

However, it is only at the end of the ninth plague, the plague of darkness, that threat of death is mentioned. The words come from Pharaoh's lips. His heart is so hardened against the Israelites and his patience (what there was of it to begin with) worn so thin that when he sends Moses and Aaron away, he tells them that if he ever sees them again that they will be executed.

It is only after Pharaoh's death threats that God calls upon the Angel of the Lord, the angel of death, to perform the tenth and final plague.

However, the Lord shows mercy to the long-oppressed slaves and Moses instructs the Israelites (and their allies) how to avoid the death of the firstborn among them.

The instructions of this original Passover night are one hurried instruction after another. The meal is to be prepared quickly. The Israelites are told to eat standing up, with sandals on their feet, and staff in hand. When the flip-flopping Pharaoh, who changed his mind after each of the nine previous plagues, gave the okay, the Israelites needed to be ready to move.

The blood from the first paschal lambs marked the Israelite door posts so that the Angel of the Lord would pass over their houses. When death arrives and Pharaoh capitulates, he makes it seem as if it is his idea to kick the bothersome Israelites out. The Egyptians are so glad to be rid of the Israelites that they give their former slaves the "riches of Egypt" for the long journey back to their ancestral homeland.

But soon (surprise, surprise) the Pharaoh changes his mind and sends his mighty army to bring his freed slaves back. The Lord leads the Israelites during the day by a pillar of smoke. At night the pillar goes behind the Israelites as fire to keep the Egyptians, the chariots and charioteers, from overtaking the Israelites.

Soon the Israelites reach the Sea of Reeds. Moses, under the Lord's instructions, raises the staff of the Lord and the waters separate. The Israelites pass over on dry land, but the Egyptians are close behind. Surely the run-away slaves will soon be killed, or returned to slavery in Egypt.

Moses raises his staff again and the waters return. All of Pharaoh's chariots and charioteers drown in the sea. The Israelites witness the destruction of their enemy who is now powerless to pursue them. They are finally safe, but there is no going back.

In a spontaneous moment of celebration, Miriam grabs a tambourine and leads the Israelite women in a song that some scholars believe to be the oldest recorded text in the Bible:

> Sing to the Lord, for he is gloriously triumphant;
> horse and chariot he has cast into the sea.

REFLECTION ON MIRIAM AT THE SEA OF REEDS

One could make the argument that the Israelites' forty years in the wilderness were a long series of daily threshold crossings. Certainly the first threshold came when they passed under the doorposts of their Egyptian houses, marked with the blood of the paschal lambs. So what makes the crossing of the Sea of Reeds so remarkable that it causes the spontaneous celebration of Miriam and the Israelite women?

The days between the Passover and the Sea of Reeds were a fury of frenzied action. They ate a hurried meal and raced into the desert. The nighttime offered no rest as Pharaoh's chariots waited just beyond the Lord's pillar of fire for their chance in the darkness. Danger and death were ever at the heels of the recently freed Israelites.

When they reached the Sea of Reeds, all must have seemed lost. They found themselves trapped between the water and the soldiers. At the darkest hour, God opened up for them a miraculous threshold across the sea. What of the Egyptian army hot on their heels, the chariots and charioteers? God slams the threshold shut in the faces of their pursuers.

What marks the Sea of Reeds as the first important threshold is that it is the moment of no turning back. The next few decades turned out not to be easy for the Israelites. Their complaining started almost immediately after the crossing of the Sea of Reeds. However, the Sea of Reeds marks (more certainly than any other moment) the transition between the Israelites as Egyptian slaves and the Israelites as God's freely Chosen People. A new stage in the lives and journey of the Israelites arrived at the Sea of Reeds. Miriam acknowledges it with her celebration.

On our pilgrimage to Ireland, Christine and I encountered many thresholds. We crossed the first leaving Seattle. The second came when we visited Sacramento and New York to say good-bye to family. When we sailed across the ocean to live in Vienna, our third major threshold invited us to new challenges. Finally, we crossed over to Galway City and claimed our residency in Ireland.

Unfortunately on the spiritual side of things, Christine and I don't have the hindsight that the Jews of the Babylonian exile had on their ancestors' Exodus experience to know when our no-turning-back moment will occur.

What we (as pilgrims) can do is keep moving forward and celebrate every new threshold.

INVITATION TO *LECTIO*: MIRIAM AT THE SEA OF REEDS (EX 15:19–21)

> When Pharaoh's horses and chariots and horsemen entered the sea, the LORD made the waters of the sea flow back upon them, though the Israelites walked on dry land through the midst of the sea. Then the prophet Miriam, Aaron's sister, took a tambourine in her hand, while all the women went out after her with tambourines, dancing; and she responded to them: Sing to the LORD, for he is gloriously triumphant; horse and chariot he has cast into the sea.

WRITING EXPLORATION THROUGH MIDRASH

Our scripture passage is the story of Moses leading the Israelites out of slavery in Egypt. They cross the Reed Sea safely and Miriam leads the women in a dance of celebration on the other side.

I invite you into a contemplation of this passage. Sit in quiet with the images. Step across the threshold of your imagination to enter the scene.

Notice as much as you can through all of your senses. Be present to the sense of excitement and danger as they cross the sea, escaping their captors. Bask in the sense of joy when they reach the other side. Are there gaps in the story that make you wonder?

Try to imagine how Moses and Miriam must each feel. They still have a long road ahead to return to the Promised Land. Yet they pause here, after this first threshold, and dance in jubilation. Engage them in a conversation. Ask them what wisdom they have for you as you cross your own threshold onto this journey.

Allow several minutes to write down your experience.

MIDRASH EXPLORATIONS

> Safely through. "Gather round, let's celebr . . ."
> Wait, what's that we hear?

Voices on the other shore. "You left us behind, don't forget about us,"
they plead.
"Let's go," the others urge.
But I cannot go forward until all of us are here.
I must go back through the deep.
The waters part with less effort this time
and I cross the threshold of the sea
to gather the lost, the frightened, the combative, the forgotten
remnant of me.

—Toni Stone

CREATIVE EXPLORATION THROUGH PHOTOGRAPHY

Your invitation is to bring your camera out into the world for a contemplative walk and pay attention to the thresholds which shimmer forth for you. They may be doorways, windows, or portals of another kind. Notice different boundaries and barriers that invite you to consider crossing over to the other side.

Follow your intuition and see where it leads you. What discoveries you make about your own inner thresholds beckon you to cross?

When you return from your journey, reflect with the images on what these thresholds reveal about your own inner crossings.

CLOSING BLESSING

Thresholds are potent places, full of the power of possibility. We embark on a pilgrimage that necessitates the crossing over of a threshold. We launch into a liminal space where time seems to shift, and things do not necessarily move along as expected.

Crossing the threshold means to embrace the unknowing which journey brings. The ultimate personal threshold is, of course, our own death which calls us to remember what is most essential and vital in our lives.

Remember

And what did you do on earth?
I descended daily into the hush—if only for a moment,

but sometimes for blessed hours at a time.
I followed the shimmering threads which lured me
into the night, full of wonder at all that was unfolding.
I opened myself wide to gratitude,
to the delight that there was anything at all,
much less pink-petaled peonies
and generous handfuls of red berries,
the incredible sweetness of things,
or the way dawn and dusk could reveal
my own new thresholds,
how a walk by the sea can change
everything,
and that I could be so well loved, and love in return,
that I could dance on earth's forest floor
and say "yes" to life from the belly of sorrow.

And what was the best of it?
I was saved by beauty again and again,
the golden glimmer of sunlight
across wet pavement revealing a luminous world,
and the stone ruins of churches and monasteries,
with their arches of ancient longing holding
ten thousand prayers, ten thousand paths to hope.

And what would you have changed?
Only perhaps to have worried less about what might come,
which never did
in exactly the way I imagined.
And to spend less time in front of screens,
offering more of myself to the elements of wind and rain and mud,
to roll with playful abandon in the wet grass, the way dogs do.

And what will you do now?
I will reach across the veil and whisper the word
"remember" to anyone who will listen.
                    —After Theo Dorgan's poem "The Angel of Days"

Chapter 4

THE PRACTICE OF MAKING THE WAY BY WALKING

All journeys have secret destinations of which the traveler is unaware.

—**Martin Buber**, *The Life of the Hasidim*

Wanderer, there is no way,
the road is made by walking.

—**Antonio Machado**, *Proverbios y Cantares*

THE WAY IS MADE BY WALKING

When you set out on this pilgrimage you may have some intentions for this time. It is good sometimes to begin with a hint of direction or a desire.

On a true pilgrimage, we soon discover that the journey has its own rhythm and momentum. We realize, if our hearts are listening, that there are secret destinations that reveal themselves as our path unfolds.

When we take off on a journey, we want to pack a map so we know where we are going. We want to have a guide which tells us which path to go and which turns to take.

The words of Machado's poem—"Wanderer, there is no way, the way is made by walking"—are the heart of this chapter's theme. We live in a world where we can always know exactly where we are and find our destination with ease. GPS guides us along the road and tells us the turns to make.

On pilgrimage, we may be tempted to bring maps with us. We may want to bring guides for the physical landscape. Plus, we might also bring along guidebooks for the inner journey and hope we might get some direction from their wisdom.

Machado's words above have been a kind of mantra for me in recent years. As my own spiritual path loosens its grip on plans and certainties, I move deeper into mystery. I'm discovering the truth that "there is no way / the way is made by walking." Sometimes, when I am working with someone in spiritual direction, I hear the longing from them to know the path God is calling them to, to have some certainty they are making the "right" choice.

This way of thinking about God is limiting. I have come to believe that God does not call us to one particular path that we scrutinize and discover. God calls us to the fullness of living which can be manifested in a multitude of ways. We have to listen closely for what is truly life-giving and there lies the struggle. We resist trusting ourselves. We tell ourselves stories about why we should stay stuck.

Following the way made by walking means listening for what is life-giving but on the inner pilgrimage also involves descending into the depths of our being. This means we must examine the places where wounds and shame dwell. We are called to retrieve these lost parts and welcome them back in to the wholeness of our being. This is why many of us never get very far. The inner voices that criticize and cajole become too loud. We return to what is comfortable, to what numbs us, and prevents us from claiming a life that is more congruent with our heart's desires.

THE NECESSITY OF YIELDING

We each have a particular way, and we are responsible for the choices we make which shape the direction of our lives unfolding. At the same time, we are also invited to yield our desire to control that unfolding. The spiritual journey calls us out into the wild places where God is not tamed and domesticated. We are asked to release our agendas and discover the holy direction for our lives.

I think "yielding" is at the heart of the monk in the world as well. Much like in my work with contemplative photography, where I invite you to consider shifting your attention from "taking" a photo to "receiving" one—a very subtle shift which can change how we see everything—we are called to yield in each moment to a greater presence at work in our lives. We must surrender our egos and our willfulness for a larger wisdom to move through us.

When we yield, we allow a holy pause, notice where we are "forcing things," and then we can let them go. It is about smiling gently at all the inner desires that attempt to grasp control of our lives. When we do, we can give those feelings a compassionate gaze. We can allow each of them to dissolve into this endless embrace, yielding to the greater force at work within us.

peregrinatio

For the Celtic monks, this metaphor for journeying was a powerful one that shaped their vision for the Christian spiritual life. *Peregrinatio* is the call to wander for the love of God. It is a word without precise definition in English and means something different than pilgrimage. This wandering was an invitation into letting go of our own agendas and discovering where God was leading.

The wandering saints who journeyed for "the love of Christ" set forth without destination, often getting into a small boat with no oars or rudder, called a coracle, and trusted themselves to "the currents of divine love." The river or sea would bring them to a place of rest they did not chose themselves. The impulse for the journey was always love.

In this profound practice, God becomes both the destination and the way. The Spirit is the companion and the guiding force. The Holy One issues the call to the journey, unfolds the journey, and greets us at the end of the journey.

After we moved to Ireland, I reacquainted myself with the practice of *peregrinatio*. While I knew the term, it took on a whole different meaning in Ireland. The ancient green hills that spawned generations of holy men and women drove the meaning of the word deeper into my soul. While we loved Vienna, being in the landscape of Ireland drew us further into our own pilgrimage.

Many people were surprised in this shift of direction, but I can look back and see clearly the movement of the Spirit at work calling us to a place where our souls and our work could be nourished in ways I couldn't have imagined. This is why the first impulse for the journey must always be love. At the time it felt like another great journey of trust and yielding to the currents carrying us forward. Now that we have landed in Galway and been here almost two years, I feel something very powerful at work that I continue to discover unfolding.

Apavia or Roadlessness

The second-century bishop and theologian St. Irenaeus wrote that the true pilgrim was to live life in a state of *apavia*, a Latin word which means "roadlessness." He called for a posture of deep trust in the leading of the Spirit, rather than human direction. In essence, he taught that the place where we don't know where we're going is also the place of greatest richness. In his book *Exploring Celtic Spirituality* Ray Simpson writes,

> They did not get their adventure from intellectual exploration, but from obedience. In this, they mirrored those personalities portrayed in the pages of Genesis who set out into the unknown in obedience to God. These Biblical travelers did not try to ensure a good result, as we are prone to do, before they set out. They achieved results not by going to people who were likely to react in a way that would bring the desired results, but through prayer. . . .
>
> The Irish monks defined the true search for God as starting from apavia (roadlessness), a state of complete trust in the direction of God rather than that of a human decision.[1]

What would it mean to embrace roadlessness in your own life journey? Where are the places you cling tightly, wanting to know the direction and outcome?

Following the Thread

There's a thread you follow
Nothing you do can stop time's unfolding.
You don't ever let go of the thread.

—**William Stafford**, "The Way It Is"

Making the way by walking, *peregrinatio, apavia*—these are all metaphors for relinquishing control and stepping forth in trust of the greater currents that carry you toward home. They are the heart of a great inner pilgrimage.

Another favorite image for this in my own journey is "following the thread." William Stafford writes about it in his poem "The Way It Is." Following the thread developed into an essential practice for me as my own journey unfolds, as I lean into the next step.

The six months we spent living in Vienna offered a beautiful golden thread to follow which revealed the meaning of that experience for me.

We moved overseas towards the end of summer. As we unpacked, two different friends sent me images of Our Lady of Czestochowa, one of the Black Madonnas found in Poland. These friends felt drawn to her and I felt drawn to receive the images they sent. My journey to Vienna became a vital part of helping heal my relationship with my father, and I felt this invitation to allow the Blessed Mother in all of her fertile darkness to be a part of that journey. Welcoming in the compassion of Mary, the one who understood suffering, offered me the solace I needed to find forgiveness toward others who had wounded my heart.

After I received these images, I had a dream. A ten-year-old girl in my care (in the dream) committed a murder. I was arrested, tried, convicted, and sentenced to ten years in prison.

I brought the dream to my spiritual director and we talked about the rage of the little girl. The conversation made me realize the little girl represented me and the rage directed at my father. We explored what it would mean to enter into the prison cell with her, live in her rage, and figure out what she could say to me. As I thought about this, I told my spiritual director about my recent encounters with the Black Madonna. He encouraged me to find one in Austria I could visit for wisdom.

Two days later I attended a new Catholic mass in Vienna. Some lovely people invited me on a pilgrimage to visit the main Marian shrine in Austria, called Mariazell. What struck me about this particular shrine to the Blessed Mother is that her name means "Mary of the Cell," which echoed my dream.

The legend tells us that a Benedictine monk walked in the forest carrying a wooden statue of Mary. After hours of walking, he got lost and cried out to her in prayer. A way through the forest opened up and he found his way out. He dedicated a prayer cell to her on the exact location. Mary spoke to me in the dream and beckoned me to the cell dedicated to her.

The next Saturday, I went on the pilgrimage. When we reached the shrine, we didn't find a simple wooden shrine. We went inside to find an elaborate altar with an imposing statue placed right above it. The wooden statue of Mary and the baby Jesus both wore bright golden crowns. The blessed mother wore a white dress with gold embroidery. Golden rays expanded outward from behind them.

The whole atmosphere seemed contrary to my dream and vision. When I knelt at the altar to pray, I heard her voice speak to my heart; *release me from these encumbrances and go find me in the forest.*

So, in the coming weeks, I did just that. I had already been finding great solace and healing in the forest, but Mary's call urged me on to spend as much time there as I could. The Vienna Woods are only a tram-ride away from the city center and there I felt peace. It was a place my father always found some peace as well.

The following week I was working with the fairy tale "The Handless Maiden" for a class I was teaching. What seized my imagination in my reading of it this time was the maiden's journey through the forest to the pear garden. I was so moved by the image of her, vulnerable and alone, having her hands cut off by her father, and finding nourishment in the gift of pears.

I discovered a poem titled "Pear" by Nan Fry, a contemporary poet about the handless maiden which describes a pear tree that leans over and offers her generous nourishment.

Her words broke something open in me, a longing I had to receive rather than to reach. I wanted to sink deeper into life's nourishment for me. I was hearing words that encouraged me to not strive and work so hard. The pear became a symbol for this.

Soon after, my dear friend and teaching partner, Betsey, came to visit me in Vienna for a few days before heading to France to help lead a pilgrimage which included visits to several Black Madonna sites. I told her of my unfolding journey with Mary and the pear. She told me that very often the Black Madonnas were carved from pear wood. I began looking on the Internet to see if Mariazell had been. I was never able to find out the wood she was made of, but what I did discover stunned me.

I found a photo of her statue without the elaborate dress she was wearing in the shrine, her unadorned beauty I had been longing to see when I visited. In her hand, beneath that elaborate dress, was a *pear*.

Here was Mary offering me the very pear I had fallen in love with from the fairy tale. Here was Mary saying in a new way, "let me bend down and offer you the nourishment you need."

After five months in Vienna, John and I traveled to Ireland for some discernment to see how the thread was calling us forward. We stopped in a cafe for an afternoon pause, a chance to talk about what we were discovering.

As we left we noticed on a display shelf that was filled with homemade jams for sale, also a large bottle. Inside the bottle was a beautifully preserved pear in brandy. I was stunned again, such an unusual way to encounter a pear. We left the cafe and walked up the street and there at the intersection only a few yards from the pear was a statue of Mary. About six weeks later we made another significant journey and moved to Ireland, where from our apartment window we could see another statue of Mary in the distance.

There are, of course, many more layers to this story, but it is a tale of thread-following, of paying attention to what is unfolding and trusting that as the direction to follow.

In monastic terms, this thread-following is about the vow of obedience for me: being obedient (which means deep listening) to whatever emerges in my life. Being a pilgrim means following wherever the call takes me, even if (and perhaps especially if) it takes me off the trajectory I expected. This is one of the places where the heart of the pilgrim and monk intersect.

Archetypal Landscapes

And you? When will you begin that long journey into yourself?

—**Rumi**, Illuminated Rumi Card Collection

Pilgrims are persons in motion—passing through territories not their own—

> *seeking something we might call completion or perhaps the*
> *word clarity will do as well,*
> *a goal to which only the spirit's compass points the way.*

—**Richard R. Niebuhr,** *Parabola Magazine*

The Spirit's compass is what we are following on this pilgrimage journey.

When we walk outside, we need to be more attentive to our surroundings. We need to see how the landscape affects our journey. Do we live in the desert? The rainforest? The Great Plains of the United States? How about a deep, dark forest? Archetypal landscapes are spaces that are meaningful to people across cultures and time. The idea acknowledges that we are shaped by the landscape we live in, and some landscapes speak to our hearts more than others.

For me, the Pacific Northwest and Ireland are such places. When John and I went to Seattle on vacation we weren't looking to move away from northern California. We just needed some rest and relaxation. Instead, we found a place we loved and could call home.

A similar thing happened on a visit to Ireland in 2007. We spent three weeks on the Emerald Isle. The landscape captured us in a way that is difficult to put into words. It went deep into our souls. We fell in love with the monastic ruins, the wide expanse of sea, the green pastures with sheep and cows grazing.

I laugh when I realize the similarity between Seattle and Galway. Both are green and misty. There is something about these landscapes that feed my soul and speak to me in a way other landscapes don't.

For example, I love taking a retreat in the desert. The barren landscapes speak to me in different ways and jar me out of my comfort zone. However, I couldn't live there because of the unrelenting sun. I need what the Irish call "soft days" when the mists shroud the landscape in a soft, comforting wetness.

Whether it's the desert or the mists, an archetypal landscape can draw us further down the pilgrim road. It can prompt us to examine our inner landscape in new and unexpected ways. The world around us helps to shape the path we take. We follow an inner prompting guided by the Spirit, but the landscape also helps shape our inner geography.

The landscapes don't always need to be dramatic. A simple garden path can help us reflect on the beauty of personal growth. An urban neighborhood can help us appreciate the diversity among different people. Each one can teach a pilgrim if she is listening with her heart.

Scripture is filled with holy encounters on top of mountains or of cave-dwellers. Moses meets God on Mount Sinai and the prophet Elijah seeks shelter in a cave while wandering the wilderness. Pilgrimage often draws us to unfamiliar places. When we go on the inner journey we might be especially attentive to seeking out new roads and pathways, unfamiliar routes rather than the usual way we travel. Our thoughts and habits have a way of bringing us on well-worn paths of action and thinking. Taking another route on an inward pilgrimage means challenging some of the routines which keep us stuck. It might be as simple as noticing the stories you tell yourself and asking if they are true.

FOLLOWING THE WISDOM OF DREAMS

> One day Alice came to a fork in the road and saw a Cheshire
> cat in a tree. "Which road do I take?" she asked.
> "Where do you want to go?" was his response.
> "I don't know," Alice answered.
> "Then," said the cat, "it doesn't matter."

> —Lewis Carroll, *Alice in Wonderland*

In ancient times, people believed that God sent them dreams as signs. They felt that God would bypass our waking life and the limits of our daylight vision. I believe that dreams help to support us in our *yes* to the inner pilgrimage. They help us make the journey our own and say yes to the gifts being birthed through us.

Joseph and Mary's invitation to a journey came by the voice of an angel in Joseph's dream. Imagine the trust this servant of God had in this kind of wisdom to follow the summons.

Put yourself in his place. The woman he was to marry finds herself with child. She claims God gave her the baby and that she didn't "know" another man. The whole community is probably laughing at him. In that patriarchal culture, his very manhood and reputation are at stake. By law, Joseph could have her stoned.

Instead, he decides to put her away in a quiet manner. This means he didn't want to expose her to public shame and possible death. He just wanted to be away from the situation without dishonoring Mary.

God sent an angel in a dream to pull Joseph further into the story. The scriptures tell us that he got up and married Mary right away. He took her into his home and on a journey he never wanted. It's not how he expected his life to unfold.

Making the way by walking is a lot like following the wisdom of dreams and night vision. This is not a journey of logic or planning. It's a pilgrimage of unfolding and ripening.

Consider keeping track of your own night and day dreams during this journey. See what signposts and guidance are offered. As you go to sleep at night, ask to receive images in the holy darkness that offer light to the path ahead.

Reflection by John Valters Paintner

THE STORY OF THE HOLY FAMILY'S FLIGHT TO EGYPT (MT 2:1–23)

Only two of the four gospels (Matthew and Luke) have infancy narratives, and they are likely the last parts of these gospels to be added. Moreover, they tell different accounts. Luke, the ever-inclusive evangelist, tells of humble shepherds being invited to the birth of the Messiah. The Gospel of Matthew, which begins with a very traditional genealogy, tells us the story of magi traveling from the East in search of the new infant king.

The magicians of Matthew, who have a bit farther to travel than Luke's shepherds, do not arrive in time for the birth of Jesus but sometime later. (This is the origin of the twelve days of Christmas and the Feast of Epiphany, with the magi arriving at least twelve days after the birth.)

Part of the magi's delay is their visit to King Herod in an innocent attempt to locate the new king foretold in the star they are following. The visit of the magi takes Herod by surprise and he consults the priests and scribes about this potential new rival. Herod, worried about his throne being usurped by an unknown baby, send the magi off as unwitting spies on his behalf.

The magi eventually find the Holy Family. They prostrate themselves before the infant Jesus and give him their gifts of gold, frankincense, and myrrh. These gifts are where we get the notion of "the Three Kings." The names, gender, and specific number of magi are never directly mentioned in the gospel. We aren't given official status, just the specific number of gifts. We aren't even given the exact number of Magi present. (There could have been only two or a fourth that simply put his name on one of the cards. There's usually at least one in every group of friends, isn't there?)

After visiting the Holy Family the magi are warned in a dream to find another route home to avoid going back to King Herod. Joseph is also warned by an angel in a dream about the danger Herod poses to his new family. So Joseph takes Mary and Jesus to Egypt, a traditional place of refuge during times of famine or danger.

The journey of the Holy Family to Egypt and back again mirrors the Israelites' journey to Egypt (with Jacob, his twelve sons, and their families) and back again (with Moses and the freed slaves). They leave the Holy Land under the threat of death (famine in the case of Jacob's family and execution in the case of the Holy Family). There are even the twin events known as the Massacre of the Innocents where Pharaoh and then King Herod kill male babies in an attempt to secure their own wicked rule. Only with the death of an evil tyrant is their safe return possible.

In the midst of this life-and-death drama, what saves the Holy Family and brings them safely back home is the simple practice of walking. Step by step, Joseph takes his family out of harm's way and back home when the way is safe.

REFLECTION ON THE HOLY FAMILY'S FLIGHT TO EGYPT

It's hard to imagine that a royal assassination decree could be thwarted by the simple act of walking away. I don't mean that to sound as if Joseph was being cowardly. The journey to Egypt proved to be a prudent, tactical retreat that allowed the Holy Family to return to the Holy Land when the time was right.

The irony of this reflection is my need for repeated implementation of this very strategy: walking away for a time. I had great difficulty writing something that I thought was meaningful and not a meandering series of tangentially related anecdotes.

After each draft, I'd reread what I had written . . . and knew that I needed to step away from the computer. In part, my desire to walk away came out of frustration. I've learned enough in life to know when a little distance and a different perspective is in order.

I've never been in such a life-and-death situation like that of the Holy Family. I don't mean to diminish the real suffering of refugees by comparing it to my writer's block. In my own small way, I know how helpful even a short walk can be before returning to a problem or task. The simple, often underappreciated gift of walking can do wonders to clear your head and recharge your energy. As an introvert, I can handle problems much better with a little time and space away from the issue.

As an introverted nester who now works online from the comfort of home, it'd be very easy for me to have very little human interaction. In many ways, it doesn't matter where I live as long as I have an internet connection. Galway is a big enough city to have home delivery for groceries ordered online. I could, theoretically, never leave my building.

For me, staying put isn't healthy. It's comfortable, but it can be stagnating. My calling isn't to be a cloistered hermit. I am called to be a monk-in-the-world and that means getting out into it.

Galway is a perfect place to do so on foot. It is the fourth-largest city in the Republic of Ireland, but the city center is made for walking. Much of the old Norman city is a pedestrian zone. It actually makes driving from one side of town to the other problematic.

It's taken Christine and me a while to get to know some of our neighbors here. Making friends as an adult is not as easy as it was when we were children. We don't have ready-made friends in the offspring of our parents' friends or coworkers.

Try running up to a stranger in a park and asking to be their friend. Actually, don't. That may not work out so well. Our American accents still mark us for tourists, even after living two years in Ireland—an understandable assumption based on the number of American tourists the locals meet in comparison to the number of Americans moving to Ireland.

And yet, slowly . . . step by step . . . we are building new lives here.

When have you needed to walk away from an issue before you could walk back to address it?

INVITATION TO *LECTIO*: THE HOLY FAMILY'S FLIGHT TO EGYPT (MT 2:13–15)

> When they had departed, behold, the angel of the Lord appeared to Joseph in a dream and said, "Rise, take the child and his mother, flee to Egypt, and stay there until I tell you. Herod is going to search for the child to destroy him." Joseph rose and took the child and his mother by night and departed for Egypt. He stayed there until the death of Herod, that what the Lord had said through the prophet might be fulfilled, "Out of Egypt I called my son."

WRITING EXPLORATION THROUGH MIDRASH

Your invitation is to enter into the scripture text with your imagination and all of your senses alive. Notice if you have expectations about how this will unfold based on your experience in previous chapters. See if you might release them without judgment and let this experience truly be a reflection of making the way by walking. Enter in without knowing where the journey will take you.

Connect to your breath and sink into stillness for a few minutes. Read the text for this chapter. You can focus on the passage for lectio divina or choose a longer passage from what comes before or after in the scriptures.

Imagine Joseph asleep and having this prophetic dream. What does it feel like to be in this ancient dream space? How does the angel appear? What feelings does Joseph awaken with? Hear the words spoken so directly and feel them in your own heart; what response does it elicit from you? What if you were told you had to protect the new life coming to birth in your own heart? Would you respond so freely?

Travel with the Holy Family in your imagination. Make the long journey to Egypt. Notice what you taste, smell, see, feel, and hear around you.

Have conversations with the angel, with Joseph, with Mary asking for wisdom on your own pilgrimage journey. Be attentive to the spaces in the story that have gone untold. The traveling, the waiting, the tending are all rich and fertile ground for you to step in and wonder how this story is your story.

MIDrasH EXPLOraTIONS

It had been a long day. There had been a lot of fuss over the visitors with the gifts. People are talking and wondering what's going on. Why is the baby so important? He has caused problems from the start. Mary being pregnant and she ran off to the hills to be with Cousin Elizabeth. Then my dream to take her as a wife, I had to travel into the hills to retrieve and marry her. We were married a few months and then word came for us to travel to Bethlehem. It was a strange night when he was born. Shepherds coming to visit, strange lights and sounds in the sky. Now this dream to leave with the child, he was in danger, if we don't move away.

Well with all that has gone before I have to take seriously this warning of harm. We said our goodbyes told people we were going home and joined a caravan of traders on their way to Egypt. In less than a year we have had a few journeys. It's time to stay in one place and reflect on all that has happened and wait for the next dream to return home.

—Seamus O'Reilly

So deep my rest as I realize he is shaking me. The babe is snuggled near my breast. "Quick!" in whispered urgency, "get up!" A dream; an angel. Yet again my whole world shifts.

Her wide eyes search out the other sleeping forms in the dim light. Family. Shelter. Laughter. Safety. Help with the babe. Witnesses. Leave these? To go where? What about the child? Her own weary body?

She nurses him, wraps him tight in soft cloths against the cold. Looks deep into troubled eyes, hugs hard—heart so reluctant to let go. Whispers: lament, blessing, prayer. She draws her cloak tight and mounts the donkey.

He walks before, she folds herself round to shelter the sleeping child. Sounds of quiet weeping fade and are overtaken by noise of hoof against stone, sheep lowing on the dark hills, a shepherd's distant snore and cough. Fierce starlight pierces the cold way.

Images and words spin and shimmer: other angels, other journeys. Elizabeth grown heavy with child, her own changing body, the midwife's voice of calm in her sea of pain, her babe's first cry, the crowded house, women cooing and teaching her the way of breast and swaddling, shepherds, more angels, strange wanders and rich gifts, terrifying whispers and other night departures.

And now they flee—alone.

What will become of us?

—Jeri L. Bidinger

creative exploration through photography

Bring your camera on a photographic pilgrimage again and embody this concept of making the way by walking in your physical journey. As you walk through your neighborhood or a nearby park, let your feet guide you. Drop your awareness out of your mind and into your body. Bring a soft gaze. Notice the impulses to turn down certain streets or pause in particular places.

As you walk, stay connected to your breath and your heart. See if you might experience this familiar place in new ways. Perhaps you go down a different route than usual. Or you open yourself to seeing things you hadn't noticed before.

Hold this image of the way unfolding before you. Open yourself to noticing symbols and images around you which speak to this. Again, there is no need to figure out the connection, just stay open to an intuitive sense of what moments have something to offer you. Try not to take the photo. Instead, you should seek to pause and receive the image as gift.

The symbols and images you discover calling to you become catalysts for deeper self-exploration. They will reveal elements of your pilgrimage to you in new ways.

Consider speaking this prayer aloud as you step out onto your photo pilgrimage: "Bless to me, O God, The earth beneath my foot, Bless to me, O God, The path whereupon I go." Imagine that each footfall blesses the earth and anoints the path you travel.

CLOSInG BLESSInG

When we make our way by walking, it demands a radical kind of surrender. It calls us to release of our desire for maps, GPS, and guidebooks. We have been invited into a deep trust of our own longings and where they will lead us. We have been called to follow the desires of God for us step by step.

Blessings in your own practice of yielding. May you discover a different path forward, one unexpected, and yet remarkably familiar.

This is what it is like to yield:

> to finally feel that place of tightness—your left shoulder,
> the crick that has been in your neck for as long as you can
> remember,
> the hard point between your eyes—soften,
> and all that is left is the
> overwhelming desire to dance,
>
> to stop resisting the endless and aching grief over a thousand
> small losses, and the one great loss of your own deepest dreams,
>
> to fall into that ocean of tears and
> find yourself carried gently to shore,

to feel the soft and trembling belly of your aliveness
turn upward toward the wide sky

as a prayer of supplication
and an act of revelation,
to tumble down a mossy meadow
blanketed with dandelions and clovers
and the golden evening sunlight
and know yourself at home,

to surrender the striving,
the grasping at what seems so important
in favor of what is
essential and true.

What would it mean to walk away from
all the "to do" lists
and commit to only one thing:
to *be*.

What would it feel like to yield your
own stubborn willfulness
which has brought you so far in
this world of achievement
and allow the things you could never have
planned for, to unfold?

I must end this poem now,
not with wise words for you to carry away
and ponder, but only this:
a reminder of that fierce and endless longing
for what is soft and supple beating in your own
beautiful heart.

Chapter 5

THE PRACTICE OF BEING UNCOMFORTABLE

SEEKING THE THRESHOLD OF TOLERANCE

Sometimes you only understand your conversation through exile, and feeling really far away from yourself and your world.

—David Whyte, *Insights at the Edge*, Sounds True Audio Interview

The disciple simply burns his boats and goes ahead. He is called out.... The old life is left behind, and completely surrendered. The disciple is dragged out of his relative security into a life of absolute insecurity ... out of the realm of the finite ... into the realm of infinite possibilities.

—Dietrich Bonhoeffer, *Cost of Discipleship*

If your journey is indeed a pilgrimage, a soulful journey, it will be rigorous. Ancient wisdom suggests if you aren't trembling as you approach the sacred, it isn't the real thing. The sacred, in its various guises as holy ground, art, or knowledge, evokes emotion and commotion.

—Phil Cousineau, *The Art of Pilgrimage*

seeking the threshold of tolerance

Part of my regular contemplative practice over the last several years involves yin yoga. This discipline practices poses that are held for long periods of time (anywhere from three to twenty minutes). The physical effect is a stretching of the connective tissue of the joints. The spiritual invitation is to go to the edge of my discomfort. I rest there to be present in my experience over time, to soften the edges, and continue to breathe. Each morning I practice, I willingly go into uncomfortable places to practice being at the edges of life.

The spiritual journeys of the Desert Mothers and Fathers offer many parallels with the path of yin yoga. These wise elders went out into the barren, lifeless desert, and sat with their discomfort. This forced them into paying uncomfortable attention to their inner life.

The wild space made them confront their temptations, distractions, and the tyranny of their own thoughts. They kept showing up until they started cultivating a sense of equanimity. They sought *hesychia*, which is the Greek word for stillness. It means more than silence or peacefulness. There is a sense in which the stillness is the deep, shimmering presence of the holy.

We each have a threshold for uncomfortable or painful experiences. When we stay within this range, we can be present to what life brings us in the moment. When we drop below our threshold we become numb and seek out things that help us avoid the pain. The numbing agents (like drugs or overwork) blind us to real healing. We reach for them when anxiety kicks into overdrive. We feel panicked, unsettled, or ill at ease.

The only way to widen our threshold of tolerance is to dance at its edges, explore uncomfortable places, and stay present. When we risk the unfamiliar, our resilience grows and we become more capable of living life.

As we explored already, the monastic cell is a central concept in the spirituality of the desert elders. The outer cell is really a metaphor for the inner cell, a symbol of the deep soul work we are called to in order to become fully awake. It is the place where we come into full presence with ourselves. We can get in touch with all of our inner voices, emotions, and challenges. God calls us not to abandon ourselves in the process through anxiety, distraction, or numbing. When we focus on Him, we can encounter Him in our deepest hearts.

Connected to the concept of the cell is the cultivation of patience. The Greek word is *hupomone*, which essentially means to stay with whatever is happening. This is similar to the central Benedictine concept of stability, which calls monks to a lifetime commitment with a particular community.

On a deeper level, the call is to not run away when things become challenging. Stability demands that we stay with difficult experiences and stay present to the discomfort they create in us.

In December 2010, a year and a half before our move, I flew to Vienna for some time of retreat. It is an ancestral place of the heart for me. Soon after I landed, I developed symptoms of a blood clot and went to the emergency room. The doctor examined me and told me she needed to run several tests. The trick came when she told me I must stay in my wheelchair and not move. If I did, the clot could move to my heart and brain. This would mean instant death.

The foreign hospital and my wheel chair became my monastic cell. The possible sickness in my body forced me to practice focusing on my inner life for eight hours. My mind moved between different states. I felt terrified I could die at any moment.

Sometimes, curiosity got the best of me as I imagined dying sooner than I expected. Sometimes, I felt a deep and abiding peace as God comforted me.

The experience turned into a profound one through monastic wisdom to guide me. I'm a firm believer that contemplative practice not only helped carry me through dark moments but it also helped calm me. My blood didn't race and chase the clot into my vital organs.

God stripped away my certainty about life and freed me from my need to control everything. I got thrust to the edges of my threshold. When I stayed, I discovered a wide open landscape within me.

Facing death freed me to risk in new ways. It taught me to fear less about what I could lose.

PILGRIMAGE AS MOVING TOWARD WHAT IS UNCOMFORTABLE

> *Pilgrimage is a journey for spiritual reasons. It comes from the*
> *Latin word for pilgrim, peregrinus, from "per-ager," meaning*
> *"through the territory." A pilgrim, therefore, is someone who*
> *leaves home to travel "through a territory" that is, by defi-*
> *nition, "not home," and so has the wider meaning of alien,*
> *foreigner, stranger . . .*
> *The pilgrim leaves home in order to experience being a strang-*
> *er—speak a different language, eat different foods, encounter*
> *different expectations—to experience otherness as the other.*

—Victoria Sweet, *God's Hotel*

We don't need to travel long journeys to grow in the spiritual life. Wherever we are, we are called to stay in the monk's cell, which means to stay present to our experience. As a culture we rarely acknowledge the value of being uncomfortable. We strongly discourage grieving people to stay with their sadness. Instead, we tell them to "cheer up" or "move on." Rarely are they encouraged to explore what grief can teach them.

We are forever seeking the next thing to make us feel good. So much of what passes for spirituality these days is about making us happy, about affirmations and having positive experiences. We so often engage in what the poet Hafiz calls "teacup talk of God" where God is genteel and delicate. Sometimes we really need these thoughts. We need to remember that we are good and beautiful.

One of my favorite books is Belden Lane's *Solace of Fierce Landscapes*, about desert spirituality. In it he writes,

> My fear is that much of what we call "spirituality" today is overly
> sanitized and sterile, far removed from the anguish of pain, the
> anchoredness of place. Without the tough-minded discipline of
> desert-mountain experience, spirituality loses its bite, its capacity
> to speak prophetically to its culture, its demand for justice. Avoid-
> ing pain and confrontation, it makes no demands, assumes no
> risks. . . . It resists every form of desert perversity, dissolving at last
> into a spirituality that protects its readers from the vulnerability it
> was meant to provoke. The desert, in the end, will have none of it.

One of the scourges of our age is that all our deities are house-broken and eminently companionable. Far from demanding anything, they ask only how they can more meaningfully enhance the lives of those they serve.[1]

Sometimes we need to be uncomfortable. Sometimes we need to remember a God of wildness who calls us beyond our edges to a landscape where we might discover a passion and vitality we never knew we could experience. We may cultivate a freedom we have never known before because our fears become something to move toward rather than away from. Developing the capacity to endure and remain open to difficult feelings is part of the movement toward spiritual maturity.

In my own life I practice this daily through yin yoga and meditation. When I stay present to experience life, I'm able to seek out what it can teach me. It helps me seek to dance at my own edges and to move toward the risky places. By staying present to the discomfort of life we grow in our resilience and our ability to recover from the deep wounds that life will offer us. We grow in our compassion for ourselves as we learn to embrace all of the vulnerable places inside of us.

Plus, as we embrace these in ourselves, we grow in our compassion for one another. We grow in our ability to experience *hesychia*—that deep presence and peace—in the midst of life's messiness and uncertainty.

I practice this through pilgrimage, by going to places where I am the stranger and sittting with my own discomfort. I stay present to the experience of insecurity in my life and see what arises from that space.

A pilgrimage is not a vacation; it's a journey of discovery. We prepare ourselves for an encounter with the holy presence which will always evoke awe and trembling.

HOLDING MULTITUDES

God turns you from one feeling to another and teaches you by means of opposites, so that you will have two wings to fly— not one.

—Rumi, *Rumi Daylight*

Our time living in Vienna was full of grace and blessing. We lived in a small apartment near the center of the city. Most days, I had moments when I felt thrilled to be there. I would wander the streets of that beautiful city and explore around each corner full of anticipation of what I might discover. I would walk around wide-eyed and gleeful, wondering how I got so lucky to live out a dream.

Some days, I would also have moments when I felt an overwhelming sadness. Homesickness would wash over me in waves as I dreamed about the familiarity of our Seattle neighborhood. Often, I would feel a deep loneliness from missing friends and family who were much too far away.

One day I walked into the pharmacy to ask for something to treat my late summer cold, and the pharmacist handed me a decongestant. He advised me to stay hydrated.

"The wine taverns would be a good place for this," he jokes. I laugh with him, savoring a moment of human connection. In that moment, I felt like I could live in Vienna forever.

Later in that same day, I called on the phone to set up an appointment with a medical specialist for a chronic health condition. My rusty German helped me enough to understand her basic instructions. However, when she asked that I do two important things before I come to my first appointment, I couldn't follow her words.

When I tell her I don't understand what she is asking she says in brusque German, "Please put on someone who speaks German."

I reply on the verge of tears, "But I am the only one here."

Nothing made me feel vulnerable like trying to navigate health systems. In that moment I wanted nothing more than to run "home" to what was familiar and understandable. She realized that she knew enough English to communicate the missing words to me: an x-ray and blood work. I sigh with relief that this hurdle had been crossed.

In my more vulnerable moments I wonder at my sanity over this continual movement between elation and discouragement. I want to feel one way so as to know what this experience is about. I want to feel one way so that I can judge whether my experience here is "good" or "bad."

Carl Jung, at the end of his life, said: "I am astonished, disappointed, pleased with myself. I am distressed, depressed, and rapturous. I am all these things at once and cannot add up the sum."[2]

While on pilgrimage, time for silence is essential. I need this anchor, this connection to Source, to remember everything that I am and to not add up the sum of my parts. In the silence, I remember that my life is not wholly good or bad here. The discomfort and the exhilaration are both essential to my experience.

Even in Ireland, where language is supposedly not a barrier, there are many sayings that are unfamiliar. There are still so many things to learn. When I learn, it pushes me to my own edges. I'm forced to notice the places where I am resistant to welcome the stranger. I want to feel stretched and expanded, but sometimes it is just *so* uncomfortable.

We are often taught that we should feel one way: happy. No one seeks to teach us how to deal with ambiguity and the contradictions in our experience. While on pilgrimage, we may fool ourselves into thinking that we should be always feeling hopeful or filled with joyful anticipation. Yet, we find that on our journey, we experience wild edges and are pushed well beyond our own boundaries.

In the gift of silence I learn again that I contain multitudes. I cannot be fully defined by happy, sad, joyful, or sorrowful. I do not need to choose, for the richness of life embraces all of it. I need only show up to each moment, to embrace the wholeness of who I am. I need only remember the wisdom of Rumi that the opposite wings of my heart offer me the possibility of flight.

SHOWING HOSPITALITY TO OUR TENDER PLACES

Once we arrived in Vienna, I felt homesickness and anticipation pulling me away from living in the moment. Plus, a part of me wanted to seize every opportunity while I was living overseas. I wanted to travel so I could see everything I could and make my present moment awareness into a sort of mountain-scaling effort of "big" experiences. I found myself daily asking what this whole experience is meant to be; "What am I here for?"

In reality, I just felt tired. This isn't surprising, considering we'd just gone through months of selling, moving, traveling, and settling a new temporary home. Not to mention the vast amounts of paperwork we needed to fill out for the Austrian government to grant John a residence permit.

Sometimes this voice inside of us pushes us to keep moving, keep adventuring, and don't slow down. If you are tired, you might miss out on something, the voices say. Yet, this journey into the uncomfortable is meant to welcome all that feels tender inside of us. In the end, it helps us to see what is true.

I found a gift in the idea of honoring my desire for rest and letting go of the idea of what "should be." I found a deep truth—the idea that a thousand present-moment small experiences will be infinitely more valuable than doing big crazy things.

A friend said something to me about "not reaching" for something but letting it happen to me. As I heard those words I felt this profound physical release in my body, a softening and an opening. I didn't even realize I was reaching until my body stopped doing it. I could feel the shift. I remembered some of my favorite words of the poet Rainer Maria Rilke: "no forcing and no holding back."

I am still on a journey that feels like it may be one of the most important things I have ever done. I am on a path of radical unknowing awaiting the gifts of this experience. Yet the call, I am certain, is to stop reaching, forcing, and trying to make the experience into *something*. I need to recognize that it already *is* something. My willingness to be here and follow the quiet voice is enough. The angels of grace know my intention is true.

The more I grasp for the clanging bells of great epiphanies the more they retreat from me. In my quiet moments of prayer, I discovered the invitation on my pilgrimage is to sit in stillness and listen to what is happening. When I did, I started to receive the treasures from my dreams, to become aware of my places of bondage, and to allow the tears to flow freely through me, all while embracing that I know what none of it "means."

I welcomed in my sweet tiredness and gave myself the gift of generous rest. I learned to ignore voices which want me to push forward in both work and pilgrimage that would give me some imagined stature. I welcomed in the tender grace of unknowing and gave myself over to fertile darkness, despite the fears or voices that long for certainty or the ones which think they have already got it all figured out. I welcomed the profound love for myself and honoring of truth I received.

What are the uncomfortable parts calling to you for some welcome? What are the voices which hold you back from this generous act of hospitality?

THE Practice OF GETTING LOST

When the safety net has split, when the resources are gone,
when the way ahead is not clear, the sudden exposure can be
both frightening and revealing. We spend so much of our time
protecting ourselves from this exposure that a weird kind of
relief can result when we fail. To lie flat on the ground with the
breath knocked out of you is to find a solid resting place. This
is as low as you can go. You told yourself you would die if it
ever came to this, but here you are. You cannot help yourself
and yet you live.

—**Barbara Brown Taylor**, *An Altar in the World*

We live in a world governed by GPS systems. At any given moment, we can know our coordinates. We've abandoned the sacred art of getting lost and of the discoveries we make when we stray from the marked path. What happens when we have to rely on our inner compass?

Barbara Brown Taylor describes the holy art of getting lost in her book *An Altar in the World*. In my favorite chapter of the whole book, she states that going on pilgrimage means releasing our tight hold on our maps and certain directions. It means we must wander across the harsh landscape being willing to be changed by it.[3]

How might you make opportunities to get slightly lost? Perhaps you could plan to go someplace new and just follow your intuition to unexpected places. When John and I travel, some of our most wondrous experiences happen when we just wander.

When we were in Vienna, we walked up a street we'd never traveled and found the Globe Museum. The beautiful gallery contained the largest collection of antique globes anywhere in the world. Sometimes in my own neighborhood I try to stray from my usual walking path to see what discoveries I might make.

Getting lost is inherent to the wilderness experience. Ending up in a vulnerable place or situation is what we are courting. We allow ourselves to lose control over the situation.

When we walk toward what is uncomfortable we increase our capacity to be with difficult experiences. Practicing getting lost actually nourishes our compassion and our ability to ask for help from others. Notice when you rush to pacify the anxiety of being vulnerable. Can you just allow yourself to be with the uncomfortable feelings without having to fix them or change them in any way?

What are some other ways you could practice getting lost? Perhaps disregarding the performance indicators at work or the latest trends in reading or clothing? Sometimes getting lost means rejecting the status quo, the way or path that society tells us is valuable.

journey of strangeness and exile

Help me to journey beyond the familiar and into the
unknown.
Give me the faith to leave old ways and break fresh ground
with You.
Christ of the mysteries, I trust You to be stronger than each
storm within me.
I will trust in the darkness and know that my times, even now,
are in Your hand.
Tune my spirit to the music of heaven and make my obedience
count for You.
Amen.

—A prayer inspired by St. Brendan of Clonfert

You have been invited into discomfort this week, and in that wandering to listen deeply to the guidance of the Spirit. There are no established paths to follow. We have considered the sense of invitation and the joy that comes with following our hearts toward this new landscape, but today we also deepen our consideration of the challenges of this path.

Pilgrimage is demanding as it pulls us away from what is safe and familiar. Moving us out of our comfort zone, this practice calls us to intentionally open ourselves to becoming a stranger. We are stepping towards the intentional journey into exile.

We remember again those ancient desert monks wandering out into the harsh and barren landscape. They sought this strangeness as essential to the spiritual path. Our path can lead us to strangeness and we might find God standing at the end.

It is precisely in this place of absolute vulnerability that a wider and wilder God can be encountered. Exile calls us to soften our hard defenses, to acknowledge that we don't have all the answers, to seek the resources available in our new community and reach out to strangers for support.

Thomas Merton described the journey of becoming a monk as one where we become "a stranger, an exile. We go into the midst of the unknown; we live on earth as strangers."[4]

DON'T FOLLOW THE NUMBERS

Several months back I walked down the road in Galway trying to find the office of an osteopath. The house number was 45, but after I passed 42 the numbers jumped up to 50 and continued up from there. I stopped and asked a woman getting out of her car if she knew. "Oh, don't go by the numbers, love," she said in her charming Irish accent. She proceeded to give me directions to where I needed to go (another block away as it turned out).

I laughed to myself at her comment. Here in Ireland, not only do they drive on the opposite side of the road, but all of the light switches in our apartment work in the reverse of my expectations as well (needing to be flipped up to turn off). Fries are called chips, and chips are called crisps. Most roads don't have street signs, and the numbers don't always go in order.

This is at the heart of why I embarked on this pilgrimage—to throw off my usual expectations of how the world works so that I might see new paths forward. Traveling in new cultures forces us to see things differently, so that even the smallest of exchanges carry new meaning; as Robert Bly writes in his poem "Things to Think," to "think in ways you've never thought before." As I see my outer world so attached to things being a certain way, I can begin to see this at work in my inner world as well.

Reflection by John Valters Paintner

THE STORY OF THE SAMARITAN WOMAN AT THE WELL (JN 4:4–42)

Early in his ministry and shortly after gathering the Apostles, Jesus leaves Judea to return to Galilee. Along the way they pass through Samaria. While the disciples go into town for supplies, a Samaritan woman comes out to the well where a tired Jesus is waiting. When the woman goes to draw at the well, Jesus asks her to give him some water.

The woman is taken aback by Jesus' request. She demands to know why a Jewish man would ask anything of her, a Samaritan woman. Cultural norms and a long-standing feud would normally keep these two people worlds apart, even standing next to the same well. The Samaritan woman even tries to school Jesus on the history of the well and its religious significance to her people.

Jesus' response is to tell the woman that he can offer her "living water." The Samaritan woman asks for this water right away so that she may no longer thirst, but Jesus tells her to go fetch her husband.

When the woman says that she has no husband, Jesus proceeds to tell the woman her life history, including the other men she has lived with over the years. He tells her of a time to come when Jews and Samaritans will not worship God in separate places. When she mentions what she knows of the Messiah to come, Jesus tells her that he is the one of whom she speaks.

The Apostles return at this moment and are shocked to find their new master in conversation with a Samaritan woman! They immediately question Jesus and the Samaritan woman to learn why they would dare to speak to one another.

While Jesus attends to his disciples' anxious discomfort, the Samaritan woman returns to the town. She tells her fellow Samaritans about Jesus and her encounter with him. On the strength of her testimony alone, many Samaritans come to believe that Jesus is the Messiah.

REFLECTION ON THE SAMARITAN WOMAN AT THE WELL

This gospel tale is full of confusion and culturally uncomfortable situations.

For a group of first-century Palestinian Jewish men to cross through Samaria was odd enough. Often Jews would travel out of their way to go around rather than through the Samaritans' territory. Jesus decided he needed a bit of time away from his new disciples. Was he in need of quiet or was he waiting for the Samaritan woman?

As many of you may have read or heard from other analysis of this story, it's odd that this woman comes to the well at midday and alone. It indicates that she's an outsider in her own town, ostracized by the other women.

The interaction between Jesus and the Samaritan woman is awkward. He shouldn't be speaking to her. She shouldn't be talking back to him. But I do like how she deems it necessary to explain the religious significance of the well. She's clearly not a stupid woman (she's knowledgeable in historic and religious matters) and not a demure wallflower.

Jesus confronts her with her own personal history. The Samaritan woman is living with a man but is not married to him. This is not the first time that's happened. Perhaps this is the cause of her outsider status amongst the other woman of the town.

This does not end their conversation. Out of this uncomfortable encounter comes a profound story of conversion and evangelization. Long before the Apostles seem to "get it" when it comes to Jesus as the Messiah, this Samaritan woman is preaching and converting her town to be his followers. I'm betting this involved more than a few awkward encounters.

I love how Jesus just dives into the awkward situation and initiates the conversation. It reminded me a bit of a talk I had with a friend several years ago. It was a delicate subject I had to broach and I didn't want to offend her. My attempts at diplomacy were making things worse. Finally, she interrupted me and said, "John, we're friends. Just say it and I'll let you explain it after."

Avoiding the uncomfortable things in life usually buys you more time but at the cost of greater discomfort later. I'm no fan of the "no pain, no gain" motto (it seems like a good way to push oneself to injury), but discomfort is part of growth.

Being a pilgrim is walking into a strange land and asking the uncomfortable question.

INVITATION TO *LECTIO*: THE SAMARITAN WOMAN AT THE WELL (JN 4:7–9a, 10)

A woman of Samaria came to draw water. Jesus said to her, "Give me a drink." His disciples had gone into the town to buy food. The Samaritan woman said to him, "How can you, a Jew, ask me, a Samaritan woman, for a drink?" . . . Jesus answered and said to her, "If you knew the gift of God and who is saying to you, 'Give me a drink,' you would have asked him and he would have given you living water."

WRITING EXPLORATION THROUGH MIDRASH

We arrive again at the threshold of another sacred story which invites us into its landscape. Again, we lay aside our theological interpretations and our biblical criticism. We are to simply enter the story as if it were our own, as if it were written just for us in this moment of our lives (which is true for each one of us—the beauty of the scriptures is this archetypal reality).

Close your eyes and imagine yourself stepping into the scene. See yourself at the well, with Jesus and the woman of Samaria both approaching. Experience the day, notice what you smell, taste, hear, and feel. Notice the sights around you. How do Jesus and this woman both look to you?

Pay attention to the open spaces in the story once again. Find the cracks, the lost voices, and step inside to flesh things out. Ask the questions which you long to ask. Listen for the words in response and the words beneath the words.

Have conversations with Jesus and the woman. Imagine yourself speaking from their perspectives, or the voice of the well, or of a creature nearby.

Let your imagination have free reign and see what story unfolds. As Jesus and the woman each cross boundaries to meet one another at this holy place, what wisdom do they have for your own journey into what is uncomfortable?

When you have finished, spend some time writing the scene that emerged.

MIDRASH EXPLORATIONS

> No shade, open square
> Sand blows over hot cobbles
> The water shimmers.
>
> —Caroline Moore

> His presence was deeper than the well. My spirit was refreshed by his words, I had not noticed how parched it had become. Yes, I still have to do my daily chores and the sun still beats down relentlessly but that experience remains like a spring of clear water gushing forth inside me—is this what he meant by living water?
>
> —Felicity Collins

CREATIVE EXPLORATION THROUGH PHOTOGRAPHY

I invite you again onto a contemplative walk, a photographic pilgrimage, where your only agenda is paying attention to what unfolds, listening to where you are being led.

Keep in mind the practice of getting lost and see if you might take an unfamiliar route this week. What are the safe paths that you stick to? How might you move beyond your comfort zone and take the risk to get lost this week?

When you find yourself lost see if you can stay attentive to your inner experience. Being lost raises all kinds of inner fears and voices when we find ourselves immersed in the unfamiliar.

See if you might notice symbols around you that offer insight into this experience of feeling lost or uncomfortable. See which images shimmer for you as you explore the world through a different perspective.

When you return from your walk, spend some time with the images, dialoguing, asking for their wisdom.

CLOSING BLESSING

This may have been a tender exploration of the discomfort, of walking toward the edges, of staying present to your experience.

While pilgrimage may seem like a radical kind of seeking, I have come to understand it as a kind of paradox. We have to journey to places where we feel like strangers only to crack open what is already within us. This can happen on the streets of a faraway city or in the midst of daily life. The maps we cling to, the bold experiences we long to have, are those kinds of searching actually getting in the way of simply being present to the journey already happening within us?

As we come to the end of another chapter together, I invite you to let go of this endless searching and let the discoveries arrive at the doorstep of your heart.

Give up your endless searching

> Lay down your map and compass,
> and those dog-eared travel guides.
> Rest your weary eyes from so much looking,
> your tired feet from so much wandering,
> your aching heart from so much hoping.
>
> Lay down on the soft green grass
> wet with morning dew, and watch as
> the tree heavy with pendulous pears
> bends her long branches toward you,
> offering you perfection in every sweet bite.
>
> Give up the weight of knowing,
> for the reverence of quiet attention
> and curiosity, for the delight of
> juice that runs in generous streams
> down your chin.

Chapter 6

THE PRACTICE OF
BEGINNING AGAIN

Resolve to be always beginning—to be a beginner!

—**Rainer Maria Rilke**, *Rilke on Love and Other Difficulties*

Come, even if you have broken your vow
a hundred times.
Come, yet again, come, come.

—**Rumi**, Inscription on Rumi's shrine in Konya, Turkey

ALWAYS WE BEGIN AGAIN

Where are you on this pilgrimage which has called to your deepest heart? Has your commitment waned? Has your practice fallen away? Can you notice your experience without judgment?

The human heart is a funny thing, full of passion for spirit one day and then feeling lost or astray the next. We may start to berate ourselves for not being better, more committed, more diligent. In that barrage of inner voices that rise up, we often find ourselves so much further away from our heart's desire than when we began. This very act of self-judgment actually distances us even further from our deep longings for peace and rest.

Perhaps we encounter what the desert monks called *acedia*, which is translated in different ways but essentially means slothfulness and has been called the "noonday demon." Halfway through our journey we find ourselves bored. Our spiritual practice wanes when we've got high expectations about how we would be transformed and so the realities of daily life dull our commitment. We've forgotten we are even on a pilgrimage or have distanced ourselves from its demands, perhaps.

This is why we call it practice. The monks knew that the only response to *acedia* was to continue to practice. When we feel full of judgment for ourselves, the only response is to continue to practice. We can construct all kinds of ways to abandon the conscious journey and return to a life on the surface of things. These are the temptations of the heart, written about by mystics for centuries. Why should we be surprised that we confront these same struggles as well?

The soulful journey goes straight through the heart of the desert. In the middle of that parched land, where everything comfortable is stripped away, we often find ourselves wanting to run or go to sleep.

Monastic spirituality calls us to return to the practice of showing up, of being still, of opening our hearts to an encounter with the holy. In *The Sayings of the Desert Fathers* we hear this story full of wisdom, "Abba Moses asked Abba Silvanus, 'Can a man lay a new foundation every day?' The old man said, 'If he works hard he can lay a new foundation at every moment.'" And also this story: "Abba Poemen said about Abba Pior that every single day he made a fresh beginning."[1]

The desert monks practiced what the Buddhists call "beginner's mind." Benedict describes his own Rule as a "little rule for beginners," and invites the wisdom that always we begin again.

Pilgrimage is a place of new beginnings. No matter how far I stray from my practice, there is always an invitation to begin again. Not just each day, but each moment offers us the chance to lay a new foundation.

There will be days when we don't feel like coming to the meditation mat or a quiet corner to rest and listen for guidance on next steps.

There will be days when life seems to actively conspire against peace and we start to believe that the stillness just isn't possible for us. We think that our lives are too full to cultivate genuine presence. This is *acedia* talking, a kind of inner dialogue that sabotages our sincerest efforts. When this happens, and it will happen, our invitation is to notice this and start over. We bring an inner fire back to our practice, we commit to showing up again.

This is the essence of humility, an essential monastic virtue. We are to remember that we are always beginning in the spiritual life. When we think that we have it all "figured out," the further we are from the spiritual path.

Humility demands that we always come to our journey with a spirit of openness, knowing that there is always more to learn. Conversely, when we think we've fallen away too far to return, we are also doomed to never try at all. The path of humility is about holding these two dimensions in balance. We need to discover more and begin again when we stumble. When we reject both of these, we have lost our way completely.

Committing to a spiritual practice is in part about letting go of the ego's power over us. Without even realizing it, we often begin a regular prayer practice with self-centered motives that are often unconscious. We want to be special or feel good about ourselves. We think we have the antidote to living in the modern world. Over time, however, these motives will be revealed through practice and our ego will experience disillusionment. We will want to walk away.

In *Listen to the Desert*, Gregory Mayers writes that it is the very times that we want to quit our spiritual practice that we find the essence of the Desert Fathers and Mothers. When we're plagued with dissatisfaction, we find the turmoil in our hearts that we might miss in our busyness. In these times, we recommit ourselves and start over. As Thomas Merton wrote, "There are only three stages to this work: to be a beginner, to be more of a beginner, and to be only a beginner."

I encourage you equally to be gentle with yourself in the days ahead. Remember that transformation takes a risky commitment to showing up for God. When your practice falters or slips through the cracks of busyness, remember the monk's and pilgrim's practice of always beginning again. We come back to the practice of the beginner. As we do, we can meet life again, free of our expectations. Our tendency is to belittle ourselves when we lose the rhythm of our commitment. We should seek instead to embrace starting over with joy.

As creative people, we are filled with the best of intentions. We are inspired with big visions and a longing to express ourselves in the fullest way possible. We begin a project—whether writing a book, painting a canvas, composing a song, planting a new flower bed, or starting a new project at work—with enthusiasm and full of confidence.

Somewhere along the way, our energy starts to wane and our creative inspiration becomes a source of frustration. It hangs over our head as a symbol of our failure as an artist.

Each morning ask where you need to begin and start there with humility, compassion, and with holy anticipation. Everything else follows this.

A MEDITATION PAUSE

Allow some time to reflect back on your pilgrimage commitments. What did you hope for in this time? Can you bring your heart and soul back to the work? Don't just dismiss things because you feel "behind." This is the story we create to keep ourselves from completing something rigorous but meaningful.

What are the circumstances of life that seem to conspire against your best-laid plans? What are the thoughts which rise up in response? What are the judgments you hold about yourself in response that then seek to sabotage your ability to re-commit to the journey?

Just notice these without judgment. Connect with your breath and allow it to be slow. Savor a few minutes of silence, drawing your awareness down to your heart center, and rest there in the infinite source of compassion. Bring that compassion to yourself.

Hold yourself lightly, perhaps even seeing the humor in your patterns. Humor is rooted in the Latin word *humus*, which means earthiness and is also the root of the word humility. Acknowledge that you are human. When we avoid the basic fact, we lose touch with our deepest desires. Embrace your imperfections as the landscape of your journey, the detours that take you onto other paths that aren't your own.

From this compassionate, humorous, and humble place, make a commitment to begin again. Make a promise to lay a new foundation in every moment as best as you can. When you fall away from your commitment again, return yourself to it over and over. Let your breath kindle the fire and heat within you necessary to keep showing up. Allow your pilgrim practice of beginning again to become your life practice.

LIFE AND DEATH IMPULSES

The book of Deuteronomy (30:19) says: "I call heaven and earth to witness against you today that I have set before you life and death, blessings and curses. Choose life so that you and your descendants may live."

We have a life impulse and a death impulse. Each choice allows us to move toward the things which bring us life. If we don't choose the path of growth, we can move toward that which drains us of life.

The challenge is that these two principles are sometimes hard to distinguish. I can be so easily seduced into believing that what is destructive is really life-giving. For example, when I am tired I am inclined to spend hours in front of the computer watching silly shows and believe that I am resting. There isn't anything wrong with watching TV or movies. Still, they aren't renewing our bodies and souls. When we use them to numb rather than really replenish, they become a problem. We wonder why we are so drained all the time.

Our life impulse calls us into community with ourselves, with others, and with the divine. This life impulse leads us to nourish ourselves well, knowing that this beautiful body is the vessel for our work in the world. It is essential to treat it with the profound dignity it deserves. We are grounded in our wholeness and make choices from this place. Our life impulse calls us to continue the difficult yet soulful journey we have begun. It calls us to remember the invitation whispered and reminds us the path is still waiting.

Our death impulse pulls us to retreat from the world and separate ourselves from others through dividing ideas. It is those moments when we identify with St. Paul's words to the Romans: "I do not understand what I do. For what I want to do I do not do, but what I hate I do" (7:15).

Our death impulse leads us to numb ourselves through poor quality nutrition, through mindless television programming, and through always feeling betrayed by life. We withdraw into our woundedness and make choices from this place. We lash out at others or internalize this and continue the hurtful pattern. This is a different movement than the nourishing withdrawal into silence we sometimes need. Intention is key.

At any given time, we are usually operating from both impulses. We are human. We feel tired or lonely, rejected or angry. We also experience profound joy, delight, spontaneous laughter, and deep compassion.

The call of the pilgrim is to stay awake to our own patterns of life and death. When we experience the death impulse arising, we can reject this part of ourselves and push it further underground. However, we need to feel that we can turn toward it with compassion and recognize our own humble struggles.

This doesn't mean we embrace the direction it wants to take us. Rather, we meet it as a fundamental part of ourselves. This is the first step toward transformation. The pilgrim's and the monk's path is to always begin again, even when we keep falling back to sleep.

The call is to give ourselves again to the impulse toward life. Remember that what is fruitful and life-giving is what nourishes us for the great work we each need to do. Giving ourselves to the life impulse engenders itself. The more nourished we are the more we seek out what feels nourishing. The more depleted we are, the less able we are to make wise choices on behalf of our own deepest care.

I am listening to this call to the life impulse as I move forward on my own unfolding journey. This listening is how I am being led to a life that is replenishing and full of sweetness for me. This leads me to a deeper service of others. Listening for how I might offer myself nourishment beyond my limited imagination strengthens my capacity to give. I want to create spaces where people can follow their own life impulse and learn to recognize the death impulse at work.

Where is your life impulse, your own greening flourishing, calling you? How might you meet the death impulse in you with some tenderness and compassion?

Reflection by John Valters Paintner

THE STORY OF THE PRODIGAL CHILD
(LK 15:11–32)

In the midst of a series of similar stories from the Gospel of Luke, Jesus tells perhaps one of his most famous parables, the story of a wayward child and a forgiving parent.

The younger of two brothers demands his inheritance. The father, for unexplained reasons, concedes and gives his younger son his inheritance. The young man gathers his wealth and leaves.

It doesn't take long for the reckless young man to go through a small fortune on loose living. The younger son runs out of money just as a famine strikes the land and his situation becomes tenuous. He is reduced to tending unclean animals and eating their scraps.

In desperation, the young man determines to go home and beg his father for forgiveness. His best hope is to live as a servant in his old home where he had once been a favored son.

As the young man draws near to his childhood home, he rehearses what he will say. His father, who appears to have been keeping watch for him, runs to him and embraces him. The young man's practice speech about giving up his right to be called a son for a menial job as a servant is brushed aside.

The father calls for the servants to adorn his once lost son with new clothes and jewels, a fatted calf is slaughtered, and a party is ordered in celebration. All is forgiven and a fresh start is in store for all.

Except . . .

The young man's older brother is outraged at his father's easy forgiveness and at the extravagance of the celebration. The older brother is clearly jealous of the gifts his younger brother received upon his return. He stayed behind and worked hard all those years for his father without even a small celebration for reward. The father tries to console his eldest son and invites him to join in the celebration of his brother's return.

REFLECTION ON THE PRODIGAL CHILD

As someone who grew up in a very religious family, this is one of the parables that I struggled with when I was younger. I felt stifled by a strict upbringing while others could enjoy a more carefree youth. I had a similar reaction to the parable of the workers in the vineyard from Matthew 20, sympathizing with the workers hired first who worked all day but earned the same as the workers who only worked a short while. Why couldn't I be wild and decadent? Why couldn't I have a bit of fun and seek forgiveness later?

Looking back on it now, I was whiney and ungrateful. As I matured I learned to sympathize with each of the characters in these stories. The young son may have had his fun for a bit, but at what price? He could just as easily have died as a result of his selfish greed. The workers hired later, surely they spent the morning worried about how they would feed themselves and their families. They could just as easily have starved due to lack of work.

Back in my childhood, I failed to see the blessings of a caring family or the security of steady work. The older sibling may never have been given a grand party with his friends. However, he never lacked for a roof over his head, food on the table before him, or the love of his family at his side. Why couldn't the older son (or me for that matter) have been as joyous about his brother's return as his father was? Why didn't the first workers—or I, again—feel happy for the other workers' good fortune?

In 1 Corinthians 13, Paul writes of love not being jealous. It's a passage often read at weddings. I don't think Paul, a first-century Palestinian Jew who was in favor of celibacy for any who could handle it, was writing about romantic love. Paul addressed a faith community in crisis, in part, over petty jealousies.

Forgiveness and gratitude are not limited resources. I don't get less of them if you get more. They grow and multiply when shared. That is what the forgiving father is rejoicing—his lost son has returned. Everyone's life is better for it.

We can react as the older son does and hold on to past grudges. It will destroy us in the end. However, it's always better to react as the father does and celebrate the chance to begin. We can judge ourselves for falling away and refuse to welcome ourselves back to the practice. The better option is to remember there is more than enough grace for us in our wanderings.

INVITATION TO LECTIO: THE PRODIGAL CHILD (LK 15:23B–24)

"Then let us celebrate with a feast, because this son of mine was dead, and has come to life again; he was lost, and has been found." Then the celebration began.

WRITING EXPLORATION THROUGH MIDRASH

We invite you again into the heart of the text which serves as our guide: the Prodigal Child.

Begin with some time to center yourself. Breathe gently and deeply, letting go of distractions as much as possible. Return to your heart, the place of receiving rather than analyzing, so that the story becomes a gift rather than something you need to figure out.

Read the story again and imagine yourself stepping inside. Experience it with all of your senses. Notice the gaps and spaces which invite questions and curiosity. Allow yourself to encounter the characters and dialogue with them. Write a description of the feast from your perspective. Have a conversation with the father and sons. Ask for their wisdom on beginning again on this pilgrimage.

Be aware when you want to censor yourself. See if you can offer permission for free exploration. Find out what arises from this fertile space.

Spend some time following your meditation writing down your experience.

MIDRASH EXPLORATIONS

I am the older daughter. The good one. The one who cleans the baseboards. I take out the trash and tidy the kitchen. I send cards to grandma. I am frugal with my spending and cautious with my habits. I stop after two glasses of wine, avoid pesticides, moderately support radical causes.

I weave casual celebrations into my life, small and simple pleasures, raw vegan gluten-free sugar-free organic smoothie treats with a generous tip. These celebrations are really an extension of health-care and self-care, to avoid burnout, to lead a more perfect and balanced life, so I may continue to give. I read Yes! Magazine and watch Democracy Now. I do not own a television and am always asleep by midnight.

My younger brother, though, makes me livid, livid, livid. He is sloppy, disrespectful, and sometimes cruel. He spends recklessly, extravagantly, and immoderately. He makes jokes about my cousin's early labor, says insensitive things about my uncle's cancer, and never gets his homework in on time. Why can't my mother be more strict? How can he get away with it all? My care and caution is rarely praised. This was always the avenue I saw to secure well-being, to stay in good graces.

My brother's friends love him more, my mother loves him more, because of his careless words, because he "tells it like it is." My mother worries that a challenging education could crush his spirit. Being around him causes me to clench my teeth, a secret fuming. "If you think you're enlightened, visit your family," I remember. Oh, oh, oh, what is the point? Has it all been meaningless?

I enjoy tidy spaces and feeling whole. His example, though, makes me want to drink in the morning, tell off-color jokes, slip packs of gum into my pockets in the drugstore, leave without paying, and commit random acts of disobedience. Disobedience to who? To myself? If their love is truly unconditional, then I have been imprisoning myself for a lifetime, guarding my own cell door with illusions of worthiness. I clench my jaw at my brother's party. The frustration and anger cannot show. I push it down, for I cannot feel these emotions. I am the older daughter.

—Melody

CREATIVE EXPLORATION THROUGH PHOTOGRAPHY

I invite you again into a contemplative walk, but perhaps go on a familiar route to you. Maybe it is a regular walk you take in your neighborhood. But as you walk, see if you can bring new eyes to familiar surroundings. See if you might bring a beginner's heart to this practice of seeing the world around you.

Beginning again is about letting ourselves be surprised by God and encountering the familiar with holy wonder. Instead of feeling cynical or dulled because of our experience, pilgrimage invites us back to our lives, open to receiving the gifts that are present even in the mundane.

As you walk, stay open to receiving new gifts, to seeing things in a new way, to noticing something you have never noticed before. What is waiting for you to discover it, and what might it say to you about where you are on the journey?

CLOSING BLESSING

As we get nearer to the end of our journey together, we have been contemplating beginnings. Particularly the ways we are called to begin again.

How has the Prodigal One within you been called to return to the journey beckoning your heart? Is there shame or heartache that can be offered over to the healing love of the One who always welcomes us back again?

Where are the places in your own life where you feel "behind" only to then cut yourself off from receiving the gifts still awaiting you?

I offer you a poem to close our chapter about the freshness which wonder can bring and the grace of allowing our sap to rise, when our eyes have become clouded with boredom or familiarity.

How to Feel the Sap Rising

Walk as slowly as possible,
all the while imagining
yourself moving through
pools of honey and dancing with
snails, turtles, and caterpillars.

Turn your body in a sunwise direction
to inspire your dreams to flow upward.
Imagine the trees are your own
wise ancestors offering their emerald
leaves to you as a sacred text.

Lay yourself down across earth
and stones. Feel the vibration of
dirt and moss, sparking a tiny
(or tremendous)
revolution in your heart
with their own great longing.

Close your eyes and forget this
border of skin. Imagine the
breeze blowing through your hair

is the breath of the forest and
your own breath joined, rising and
falling in ancient rhythms.

Open your eyes again and see it
is true, that there is no "me" and "tree"
but only One great pulsing of life,
one sap which nourishes and
enlivens all, one great nectar
bestowing trust and wonder.

Open your eyes and see that there
are no more words like beautiful,
and ugly, good and bad,
but only the shimmering presence of your
own attention to life.

Only one great miracle unfolding and
only one sacred word which is
yes.

Chapter 7

THE PRACTICE OF EMBRACING THE UNKNOWN

Leave the familiar for a while. . . . Change rooms in your mind
for a day.

—**Hafiz**, "All the Hemispheres"

To get to an unknown land by unknown roads, a traveler can-
not allow himself to be guided by his old experience. He has
to doubt himself and seek the guidance of others. There is no
way he can reach the new territory and know it truly unless he
abandons familiar roads.

—**John of the Cross**, *Dark Night of the Soul*

Let all guests who arrive be received like Christ, for he is going
to say: I was a stranger and you welcomed me (Mt 25:35).

—*Rule of St. Benedict* 53:1–2

BECOMING THE STRANGER

The quote above from Benedict's Rule is a foundational expression of the principle of hospitality at work. I am called to welcome in every stranger who comes to the door as the face of the divine.

I love this invitation of the Rule. At its core, it means that everything that seems strange, foreign, or uncomfortable is the place where God *especially* shimmers forth.

This hospitality applies to those who arrive at the door to my outer world in terms of people and experiences I find challenging.

Equally important, I think that Benedict is also pointing us to an inner kind of hospitality. I find this principle even more vital when applied to the inner life because that is where hospitality begins.

The Sufi poet Rumi writes about this inner "guest house" with its new arrival each day including joy or sadness, anger or depression. Welcome them each in because "each has been sent/as a guide from beyond," all of the feelings I encounter that make me want to slam the door on my inner life. These are precisely the place where we are called to meet God.

Hospitality calls us to see God through risk. It shows us that God doesn't just appear in familiar faces, people who make me feel comfortable and safe. He sends us people that challenge our little worlds to make them bigger. When we invite others into our lives, it changes our view on how things should work.

As John and I live in a foreign culture, we're challenged to practice hospitality on a daily basis. Every face seems strange and speaks in an accent I can't always understand. I see those faces when I grocery shop, eat at a restaurant, or just talk to our beautiful neighbors. My limitations and responses are challenged to find the face of God in all this strangeness.

Jungian psychologist Ann Bedford Ulanov writes, "The Holy refuses to stay put in a box. These meetings with God well beyond our images of God comprise great religious moments that smash us, or open us further to the transcendent or both. Mystics write of these moments." It is the moments that break us open, that move us beyond what is conventional or familiar, that strip the illusion of safety and security from our fingers, in which we begin to plumb the depths of the holy.

Most of us don't want God on these terms but on our own. We try to domesticate the sacred into prayers and doctrines that follow our own rules. We want to understand why things happen as they do, so we create trite responses to people in suffering.

Carl Jung once said in a BBC interview that he began calling God all those "things which cross my willful path violently and recklessly, all things which upset my subjective views, plans and intentions, and change the course of my life for better or for worse."[1]

The divine is that power which disrupts everything; it is at heart a great mystery at work.

What if our pilgrimage practice courted holy disruption? What if we welcomed in everything that challenges our perspectives on how the world works, which upsets all the plans we made for ourselves and turns them on their heads? What if we embraced the unknown as sacred wisdom for the unfolding of our lives?

What if when life started falling apart, we opened our hearts to welcome in the grief and fear that arrived? What if we considered them as holy guides and windows into the immensity of God? What if all the painful feelings of loss and disorientation were invited in for tea? What if everything that turned our preconceived ideas inside out was precisely where we found God?

I do not mean to imply that everything "bad" or painful that happens is somehow part of an inscrutable plan. This again puts God back in the box. This is a way we try to control suffering; we make elaborate theologies out of our limited understanding. Welcoming in the inner experience does not mean validating the outer facts and the terrible things people do to one another.

What I do mean is that we are called to make space for the full range of our experiences of discomfort, strangeness, and loss.

What does it mean to trust that somehow the brokenness we experience can become a doorway into a more expansive way of imagining the world?

When we practice this kind of radical hospitality to all the ways holy disruption arises in our lives, we make room for the possibility that fear does not have to compel our every response. We begin to experience more kindness to everything that feels difficult within and so this begins to flow outward to others.

We no longer feel compelled to limit who might be included in the realm of God's love and we learn to let go of our own agendas. We begin to see that God is so much bigger than our own imagining and we talk with more humility. We are willing to consider that we might have been wrong all this time.

This is true of our own pilgrim journey as well. We already cultivated seeing the world with new eyes; we may be ready to see the things which enter our lives and lead us to unfamiliar places as an essential part of our own unfolding.

Many anxieties accompanied the transition when we moved to Vienna and then to Galway. We longed for home even as we tried to embrace the unknown. This has been a long and slow journey. It took some time. This is one of the gifts that threshold brings—an intimate encounter with the feeling of exile so that "home" becomes that much sweeter.

I knew moving across sea and land to a faraway place would demand much from me and break me open numerous times. However, I could never have anticipated the ways our journey unfolded and changed us. It keeps doing so, and that is the point.

WELCOMING IN DOUBT

More than eleven years ago my mother died quite suddenly. I sat with her the last five days of her life in the ICU. The dreadful and holy space of death's threshold became my monastic cell.

In the year that followed, loss-created grief filled the hollowness in my chest. The second year, I had hoped, would begin to ease the sorrow, but it soon became more intense. I dealt with not only the emptiness of pain but doubt started to emerge in my prayers. My doubts came from the place of someone who loved deeply and wanted to understand why death is woven into the fabric of the universe.

I was thrust on a pilgrimage I did not want but I couldn't avoid. The theological framework that sustained me unraveled before my eyes. I had wrestled with this question of suffering and death before, but, somehow, this doubt felt different.

The best way to describe it is that I sometimes felt like I hovered on the edge of a dark canyon. Sometimes, too, life felt unbearably sweet and beautiful. Both seemed present in my thoughts.

I am grateful that I had the support of John and friends. My spiritual director encouraged me to stay in the places of doubt and unknowing. He wisely counseled that moving toward my despair and staying present would be the only way to understand it. I would eventually walk through to the other side.

My director gave me permission in our time together to not try and figure out what I believed. He wanted me to experience what was true for me. I embraced the unknowing doubt.

Often in our church communities there is a sense that if we don't "believe" we are somehow deficient. In people's rush to alleviate their own discomfort, they encourage others who are struggling to "trust" or find "faith." I put all these words in quotes because they are notoriously hard to define. They often carry a lot of baggage with them.

In my own journey, along with the love of friends and the support of my spiritual director, I found being in nature a profoundly healing experience. Creative expression is also essential in my own journey to explore mystery. The wild spaces of creation, both inner and outer, offered me a place to be with my unknowing, to rest into mystery without having to figure things out. Wildness is hard to pin down, and that's the beautiful gift we receive from it. It offers us the unexpected when we set aside our expectations about how the world works.

The gifts of embracing doubt as a spiritual practice have been many. I've grown in my capacity to rest in the tensions of life. I question long-held assumptions. I plunge myself more into mystery. All of this grows the courage of the pilgrimage inside of me.

If we're really honest with ourselves, in a world where terrible things happen there must be room made for doubt. We must give ourselves and others space to wrestle with the essential questions of our lives. Believing in times of beauty and transcendence leads us to the idea there must also be room for something bigger than what we traditionally call faith or belief. We are shown a deeper kind of knowing, one that emerges from blood and bone, those are moments where we finally feel at home in the world and can breathe deeply.

What are the unknown shores beckoning to you? Might you yield your resistance and desire for familiarity to step into the wide horizon of possibilities beyond your understanding?

An Altar for an Unknown God

*Let mystery have its place in you; do not be always turning up
your whole soil with the plowshare of self-examination, but
leave a little fallow corner in your heart ready for any seed the
winds may bring, and reserve a nook of shadow for the passing
bird; keep a place in your heart for the unexpected guests, an
altar for an unknown God.*

—**Henri-Frédéric Amiel**, *Amiel's Journal*

John Cassian, one of the ancient Desert Fathers, describes three renunciations he says are required on the spiritual journey. The first is our former way of life as we move closer to our heart's deep desires. The second is the inner practice of asceticism and letting go of our mindless thoughts. The third renunciation is to let go of our images of God and to recognize that any image or pronouncement we can ever make about God is much too small to contain the divine. Even the word "God" is problematic because it carries with it so many interpretations and limits based on our cultural understandings.

We live in an age when fundamentalism has emerged as an overwhelming force in religious consciousness. In times that are chaotic and uncertain our human minds grasp for a sense of control. One of the ways we try to make sense of things is to engage in black and white thinking. When we try to establish clear rules of who God loves, it's a way of coping with this felt loss of shared cultural sense of meaning.

The *via negativa* or "apophatic" way in Christian tradition, which means the way of unknowing, demands that we talk about God only in terms of what God is *not*. It helps to cleanse us of our idols. Alan Jones, in his book *Soul-Making*, writes, "We can only say that God is both unknowable and inexhaustible."[2]

Humility is required. We are so attached to our ideas of who God is and how God works in the world. Ultimately, what the desert journey demands is that we let go of even this false idol and open ourselves to the God who is far more expansive than we can imagine.

Letting go of our images of God can be terrifying. Suffering in our lives exposes our previous understanding as no longer adequate to give meaning to what is happening to us.

When my mother died, many people offered trite words of shallow comfort. They didn't want to sit with me in the darkness but only hoped to rush me through to a place of light.

This is the mystical experience of the "dark night of the soul," when old convictions dissolve into nothingness. We are called to stand naked in front of the unknown. We must let the process move through us, one which is much greater than we can comprehend. We can never force our way back to the light. It is only in this place of absolute surrender that the new possibility can emerge. We don't just have one dark night in our lives. Rather, the dark nights are frequent and so is the call to release our idols of God.

As Christian mystic Simone Weil tells us, "there are two atheisms of which one is a purification of the notion of God."[3] As soon as our human minds begin to fashion categories, we risk making idols of them.

Meister Eckhart, a thirteenth-century Christian mystic living in Germany, describes the practice of *gelassenheit*, or non-attachment. Most contemplative traditions, such as Buddhism, have a version of this concept and cultivate holding life with an open palm.

In yoga philosophy, *aparigraha* means "non-grasping." We let go of how we would have life be, and welcome knowing the reality of things. This shows us how much we don't know. Just like John of the Cross, Eckhart described God as "no-thing," meaning that God is not an object we can possess but a reality that is far greater than our human comprehension.

We let go of who we think God is and cultivate openness to the One who is far beyond the horizons of our imagining. In the book of Job, God challenges Job's desire for understanding and asks "where were you when I laid the foundation of the earth?" (38:4).

God is never a set of concepts to be understood but a relationship to encounter. In this way, the spiritual life is *always* a journey. We do not let go once and for all. Instead, we move through the layers of our lives until we are living more from our hearts than our minds. We travel toward the horizon, realizing that it is always receding from our view. This is the heart of our pilgrimage.

There is a wonderful story from St. Anthony which goes like this:

> Abba Anthony said to Abba Joseph, "How would you explain this saying?" and he replied, "I do not know." Then Abba Anthony said, "Indeed, Abba Joseph has found the way, for he has said: 'I do not know.'"[4]

"I do not know" and "He has found the way." This week we discover the way is not just made by walking. We are also made by releasing everything to which we cling too tightly—our need to be right, our need to feel secure, our need to be in control. None of those are the way according to the desert and Celtic monks.

on being an outcast

> *[Abba Nilus] said, "Happy is the monk who thinks he is the*
> *outcast of all."*
>
> —*Sayings of the Desert Fathers*

You may stumble a bit over the saying above; I know I did. The monk who thinks he is an outcast is *happy*? If the monk's path being toil wasn't enough, then perhaps you are starting to wonder what you got yourself into entering this desert path.

In my book *The Artist's Rule*, I present the monk and artist as archetypes, that is, they each have an energetic presence within us and are present to people across time. I describe the inner monk as that aspect of us which seeks out a whole-hearted connection to God and cultivates the ability to see the sacred presence shimmering everywhere.

The inner artist seeks to give form to our inner longings and create beauty in the world. Both the inner monk and inner artist are border-dwellers. Neither fit neatly into mainstream society as they both call us to new ways of seeing.

The monk calls the world to presence rather than productivity. The monk takes the demanding path of inner work and growth. The world offers possible ways to distract them from these struggles. The monk chooses a simple life in the midst of an abundance of riches. When we commit to a contemplative path, we begin to let go of the things that aren't important anymore. We release the non-essentials of life that society tells us are important.

We strangers on the pilgrimage seek to embrace the unknown in service of the journey. The pilgrim journeys to the edges of the inner and outer world because we know there is more of God to be found there.

To be an outcast means that we don't align ourselves with the dominant way of thinking. It means we live on the lush and fertile edges of life (which paradoxically is also right at the heart and center of things).

Our pilgrimage might lead us to a place of deep peace and joy at not "fitting in" anymore. We can be true outcasts in the world. We might experience a sense of delight that our ways are not the world's ways but a path rooted in a deeper kind of wisdom.

Reflection by John Valters Paintner

THE STORY OF PETER'S DENIAL FORETOLD (MK 14:22–42)

Jesus enters the holy city of Jerusalem as a welcomed celebrity. He rides on a white donkey as foretold of the messiah by the prophets. His way is laid with palm branches and the crowds cheer Jesus' arrival with much fanfare. Once chased out of town, Jesus is now celebrated and welcomed.

After the crowds disperse and Jesus is alone with his disciples, they share a sacred meal. Jesus breaks bread with the inner circle. Something strange is going on at the meal. This is no ordinary Seder meal. Jesus equates the bread with his body and the wine with his blood. This must be a very strange twist for the disciples.

Then, in the midst of what should have been a celebratory dinner, Jesus announces that he will be betrayed by one of his own.

Peter is adamant about his own loyalty. Jesus confronts Peter and says that he, too, will be scattered like a lost sheep after the shepherd is struck. The "rock" restates his devotion. Even when Jesus tells Peter that he will deny him not once or twice but three times (in that very same night, no less), Peter swears he would die beside Jesus before even denying him once!

Even before Peter faces (and fails) his own test, Jesus' agony in the Garden of Gethsemane foreshadows Peter's coming betrayal of Jesus. As Jesus goes off to pray alone, he asks the disciples to keep watch with him. Peter, not realizing the gravity of what is about to happen, falls asleep. Jesus chastises Peter, but he falls asleep a second time. Even after a second rebuke, Peter falls asleep a third time as Jesus agonizes over his coming fate.

Reflection on Peter's Denial Foretold

In the gospels, Peter is the disciple who is most often portrayed as being most confident in knowing who Jesus is and is most willing to demonstrate his loyalty to Jesus. However, when the crucial time comes for Peter to stand beside Jesus, Peter first falls asleep on the job and later denies he ever even knew Jesus.

What must add insult to this injury of Peter's pride is that Jesus warned him that it would happen. But Peter is so sure that he knows himself and what Jesus said would happen could never happen. Peter comes to terms with the fact he did not truly understand who Jesus was before his death. When the test (the test he was so sure he would pass) comes, Peter fails over and over again.

But is Peter a failure or merely human? Recent research indicates that when people are faced with evidence that their long-held beliefs are incorrect, most people actually deny the evidence. They dig their heels in further to their beliefs.

There is also the Dunning-Kruger Effect that shows an inverse relationship between most people's confidence in a particular area and those same people's actual competency in that area. Even when these people are shown evidence of their incompetency, they tend to still be confident in their abilities.

Like Peter, the thing most of us tend to know the least about is ourselves.

I don't know how many times I convinced myself that I was a great teacher, only to fall short of my own expectations. In part, these failings were caused by over-confidence which led to lack of preparation on my part. Perhaps worst of all, I dismissed these failures as exceptions to the rule or due to outside factors beyond my control and not habitual problems that needed to be addressed.

On the other hand, there's the time I decided to pick up the ancient Irish sport of hurling at the age of forty. I knew that I'd never be any good. So, I just went out and had fun with it.

After a year's season, I found myself surprised at what I picked up in such a short time. Supportive teammates proved to be fantastic teachers and encouragers. I still wanted to dismiss my learned skills as "beginner's luck" or my friends as just being kind. I found it difficult to acknowledge that I had improved.

I don't mean to imply that Peter and the rest of us are idiots. We humans tend to be a bit arrogant and lack real self-awareness. We don't like criticism, even from ourselves. This makes us overly critical, especially of ourselves.

It's only when we embrace our shortcomings that we can overcome and accept them. My teaching skills improved when I accepted outside input or really took myself to task. I stopped thinking of myself as a joke on the hurling pitch and accepted the praise of those who had an objective perspective.

As monks-in-the-world and pilgrims on life's faith journey, we need to embrace the unknown. Not just the unknown "out there in the world," but the unknown aspects of ourselves. We are a great mystery, calling us to a lifetime of pilgrimage within.

INVITATION TO *LECTIO*: PETER'S DENIAL FORETOLD (MK 14:27–31)

Then Jesus said to the Apostles, "All of you will have your faith shaken, for it is written: 'I will strike the shepherd, and the sheep will be dispersed.' But after I have been raised up, I shall go before you to Galilee." Peter said to him, "Even though all should have their faith shaken, mine will not be." Then Jesus said to him,

"Amen, I say to you, this very night before the cock crows twice
you will deny me three times." But he vehemently replied, "Even
though I should have to die with you, I will not deny you." And
they all spoke similarly.

WrITING EXPLOraTION THrOUGH MIDraSH

As we explore unknowing, doubt, and mystery this week, we invite you
to step into another scripture text: the story of Peter's denial. We can
see how Jesus sees deeply into Peter's heart. Jesus knows this is a part of
Peter, even as Peter denies his capacity for denial.

Find a comfortable position and rest into your breath, find its
rhythm, and let it carry you to a place of stillness. Notice if there are
any places of tension or holding in your body. When you enter the unknown, it can create all kind of physical resistance in addition to the
emotional kind. Bring your breath to any place of holding to see if you
can invite in a softening there.

Descend your awareness into your heart center. Releasing the analytical and judging mind will be especially important this week. As we
move toward the unknown, our minds will be desperate to take control,
to figure things out, to allow only for cautious exploration. Bring compassion to these parts of self who want only to protect you from what
they imagine to be great threats to your well-being.

Step into the story from this place of open receiving. The text happens just after you shared supper with Jesus, broke the bread and drank
of the wine. What do you experience as you sit there amongst the disciples? How do you feel as Jesus says "all of you will have your faith shak-
en" with such conviction? How does Peter look as he vehemently denies
that he might be made to doubt?

Find the spaces in the story that want to be told and revealed. Have
conversations with the others gathered about their own doubts. Ask
Jesus for wisdom for entering the unknown on your own pilgrimage
journey. Pay attention to where the questions arise for you and let your
imagination fill in those spaces with story. Bless the doubts as they enter
in.

When you have come to the end of your exploration, allow some
time to write down your discoveries.

MIDrash EXPLOraTIONS

Peter: I am sure of things, this table is solid, this cup is smooth, and I won't deny Jesus. How can he say such a thing! He makes me shake inside, shake with something, it's not anger, I'm used to anger. Is it fear? All my years with him and I felt sure we were going to change the world. Now, I'm not so sure, what does he want from me? Does he actually want me to step out into the night, where I can't even see and follow him into the unknown?

—NRC Kelly

Tonight, after denying
the possibility of Christ,
I discover there is:
No answer,
No path,
No destination,
No certainty,
No figuring it out,
No home,
No possibility of arrival,
Nothing here, nothing there,
Neti, neti.
Going nowhere.

—Jan Elvee

CreaTIVE EXPLOraTION THrOUGH PHOTOGraPHY

You are invited into a contemplative walk, bringing this theme of embracing the unknown with you on the journey of seeing.

As you walk, as in previous weeks, lay aside your desire to know where you are going. Pay special attention when you're try to figure things out and pause to reconnect with your desire to embrace the unknown.

See if you might walk through the world as if it were all a liminal space. You do not know what will happen this next moment, you do not know what will cross your path, you do not know what you will experience or encounter. This is, of course, always true, but hold this awareness especially.

Notice if there are images out in the world asking you to receive them which might speak of embracing the unknown. See what shimmers forth around you offering you wisdom for entering even more deeply into the release of certainty, and the courting of healthy doubt.

CLOSInG BLeSSInG

You have great courage for staying on the path. Make the journey into the heart of the unknown. Look to embrace the strangeness and doubt. Realizing the true limits of your own horizons is profoundly humbling, but also liberating.

In Christian liturgical celebrations, Holy Week invites us into a world full of betrayal, abandonment, mockery, violence, and ultimately death. The Triduum, those three sacred days of unfolding liturgy, calls us to experience communion, loss, and the border spaces of unknowing. Holy Saturday is an invitation to make a conscious passage through the liminal realm of in-between.

I love the wide space of Holy Saturday that lingers between the suffering and death of Jesus on Friday and the vigil Saturday night proclaiming the return of the Easter fire. For me, Holy Saturday evokes much about the human condition. It helps us examine the ways we are called to let go of things, people, identities, or securities. We wonder what will rise up out of the ashes of our lives. We suffer from our pain, grief, and sorrow. We don't know if we will ever grasp joy again. I hope you see that much of our lives rest in that space between loss and hope. Our lives are full of Holy Saturday experiences.

Instead of rushing to resurrection, we must dwell in the space of unknowing. We must hold death and life in tension. One day, we can help others live through these scary and tense landscapes. The wisdom of the Triduum is that we must be fully present to both the starkness of Friday and the Saturday space between before we can really experience the Resurrection.

We must know the terrible experience of loss wrought in our world. This pain can teach us more when the promise of new life dawns, and we will appreciate its light because we know the darkness. Our pilgrimage teaches us this as well.

Much of our lives are spent in Holy Saturday places but we spend so much energy resisting, longing for resolution and closure. Our practice this day is to really enter into the liminal zone, to be present to it with every cell of our being.

Make some time today to sit with all of the paradoxes of life. Bring yourself fully present so you can live in the discomfort of the experience. Rest in the space of waiting, and resist trying to come up with neat answers or resolutions. Imagine yourself on a wild border or standing on a threshold. See yourself knowing that you cannot fully embrace what is on the other side until you have let this place form in your heart. When you notice your attention drifting or your mind starting to analyze, return to the present moment. Allow yourself to feel whatever arises in this space. Honor the mystery.

The poem I share with you today is about the desire for a God who is fluid, vast, mysterious, and full of creative possibility beyond my imagining.

Please can I have a God

Please can I have a God
> not fossilized, hardened, stiff, unshaken,
> not contained in creeds and testimonies,
> judgments and stone tablets,
> but in the wound breaking open.

Please can I have a God
> who asks me to worship at the altar of mystery,
> to lay aside certainty, and curl up
> in the hollow of a great stone down by the river,
> to hear the force of it rushing past.

Please can I have a God
> with questions rather than answers,
> who is not Rock or Fortress or Father,

but sashays, swerves, ripens, rages
at the rape of the earth.

Please can I have a God
    whose voice is the sound of a girl, long silent from abuse,
    now speaking her first word,
    who is not sweetness or light, but the fierce utterance of
    "no" in all the places where love has been extinguished.

Please can I have a God
    the color of doubt, the shape of uncertainty,
    who sees that within me dwells a multitude,
    grief and joy, envy and generosity, rage and raucousness,
    and anoints every last part.

Please can I have a God
    who rolls her eyes with me at platitudes and pronouncements
    and walks by my side in the early morning
    across the wet field, together bare-footed and broken-hearted,
    who is both mud and dew.

Please can I have a God
    who is the vast indifference of forest and night sky,
    who is both eclipse and radiance, silence and scream,
    who is everything slow and dark and moist,
    who is not measured, controlled, but ecstatic and dancing.

Please can I have a God
    who is not the flame, but the flickering,
    not bread, but the chewing and swallowing,
    not Lover and Beloved, but the making love,
    not the dog, but the joyful exuberance when I come home.

                                        —After Selima Hill

Chapter 8

THE PRACTICE
OF COMING HOME

*My final question, "How will I know when I have reached
the destination?" brings me full circle, and I face the Mystery
again. Perhaps the truth is that we never arrive, not because
the journey is too long and too difficult but because we have
been there all along. I am coming to believe that there is no
final destination except to continue to be on the journey and
to know that every place along the way is a holy place because
God is present. I believe that God is calling us to stand on our
own ground and know that it is holy and let our roots grow
deep. And yet at the same time, the journey goes on. It is a
paradox, I know, but perhaps we are traveling most faithfully
when we know ourselves to be most at home.*

—Judith E. Smith, "This Ground Is Holy Ground," *Weavings
Journal*

RETURNING HOME AGAIN

We came to Ireland full of possibility. A rainbow greeted us on our arrival, and hope filled our hearts. That isn't to say we didn't face more roadblocks and frustrations early on in our move. After three weeks, we needed to move from the village of Kinvara to the city of Galway. The resources and the poor Internet connection made it impossible to do our work in a rural area.

I often describe the artist as one who creates out of the materials given, not necessarily the materials they want. An everyday artist tries to stay fluid and flexible. She needs to stay in the invitation of the moment and embrace the dance as it comes.

Sometimes, this dance doesn't come as we would want it. This is because of the choices or limitations of others or ourselves. It's not some God-given struggle to strengthen us. Yet, the divine presence is always there in the midst, helping us to create beauty right there.

Throughout our life pilgrimage, even in the midst of the strangeness, I do have many moments of homecoming, glimpses of what Judith Smith writes about above, to see *this* place as holy. I can see moments of joy where I have said a wholehearted "yes" to the invitation to savor all of life and be aware of opportunities for exploration. This is what the pilgrim must learn, not through books or words but through a radical encounter with the home that is inside us.

If entered into mindfully and with a whole heart, each encounter on the road has the potential to transform. The pilgrim returns home not with all the answers. Instead, they receive better questions; questions that bring the pilgrimage experience into daily life and reveal depth in all they see around them.

THE LONGING FOR HOME

We arrive at the ground at our feet,
and learn to be at home.

—**Wendell Berry**, "A Spiritual Journey"

Ultimately the pilgrimage leads us back home again. We always return bearing gifts for the community. We are always called back to share what we have been given with others. This will look different for each of us.

We are also called to a new relationship to "home." A couple of years ago I became aware of a pattern of mine. In this particular instance, I'd been away from home for three weeks teaching classes. Normally, I didn't stay away from home that long.

I usually get homesick after just a week away. This time, however, that didn't happen. Something shifted. I missed home, but my longing for home didn't pull me away from my experience.

Ultimately, I think we all long for home. Certainly *The Wizard of Oz*, that great archetypal film, invited us to remember that the power to go home is always with us. While some physical places and landscapes feel more like home to us, ultimately it is in service to us discovering the primal home within each one of us.

What would it be like to move through the world and, no matter where you found yourself, to recognize yourself as fully at home?

TRUE HOME

The pilgrim heart seeks a peacefulness of belonging that is also a restlessness. It may feel anything but peaceful. The paradox is that there is not soul-peace that is not also unrest; there is no family that does not include strangers; there is not true home that is not a world-home.

—**Sarah York**, *Pilgrim Heart*

As we near the end of this book, ponder the paradoxes offered in the above quote. Can you allow yourself to hold both these things together: peace and unrest, family and strangers, true home and world-home? What does each of these invitations mean for you in this season of your life right now? What are the paradoxes of the spiritual life you are being called to hold in your being?

Allow some time today to be with your own expectations about where you "should" be at this point on the journey. Are you expecting some grand revelations? Were you hoping for clear answers? Did you have a vision for what "home" would look like? Can you release any thoughts about what the journey is supposed to look like and allow yourself to be where you are?

What if the journey has brought you exactly to this moment, full of everything you need to go home to yourself? Every journey has unfinished elements, more beasts to tame, more treasures to seek. When we return from pilgrimage we come home in a new way; we bring gifts for those who have awaited us.

THE JOURNEY CONTINUES

The point of traveling is not to arrive but to return home laden with pollen you shall work up into honey the mind feeds on.

—R. S. Thomas, "Somewhere"

Even though we are at the end of this book, the journey continues. You are called to stay on the path. Rumi describes the pilgrim way as not being for "brittle, easily broken, glass-bottle people." This path is for those courageous enough to face into the lies they have been living in service of discovering the deepest kind of truth.

As you continue forward, remember your companions along the way. Remember those who have traveled alongside of you as well as the thousands of souls who have traveled ahead of you and those still to come. You might even see their footprints on the road.

Consider how you might stay with a caravan of kindred spirits to support you in the ongoing pilgrimage of life. Look for a wise spiritual guide or a small faith community. Explore the answers found by those who came before you, as they wrestled with the same big questions of life.

As R. S. Thomas writes, the point of all this traveling is not to "arrive." The moment we think we have arrived somewhere in this lifetime is the moment we have fallen deep into the wilderness of self-delusion.

Return home in these coming days carrying this image of the pollen you have received during this time that you can transform into honey. What is the sweet nectar that will continue to sustain you? What are the practices which you commit yourself to in the days ahead?

SING A REDEDICATION OF YOUR LIFE

Now it is time to sit quiet
alone with You
and to Sing
a re-dedication of my life
in this Silent
and overflowing joy.

—Rabindranath Tagore, "A Moment's Indulgence"

I received the poem above when I attended a silent retreat a couple of years ago at a retreat center in Austria called Die Quelle, a name that means "The Source." The words called us to sit in silence by the side of God, the Source, and the ground of Love. Silence is not an absence but a profound kind of presence, a pathway into a deep communication. I attended the retreat soon after my arrival in Vienna, and so I was feeling acutely the distance from "home."

"Sing a rededication of my life" is a line from Tagore's poem that shimmered for me thoughout the week. When I read those words, I knew that was why I'd come to this place: to rededicate myself to this path, to deepen into stillness, to commit again to the contemplative way in the midst of life. This is why we embark on pilgrimage, to rediscover what it is we already know most deeply within ourselves. This is a kind of coming home.

The first two days of the retreat challenged me as I settled into the rhythm of the place. I tried to find my way among fellow pilgrims, and as I quieted enough to hear the thoughts clamoring for my attention, the level of self-judgment and criticism took me by surprise. The inner noise of old critical voices rose up with their deafening noise. Thankfully, I'd been on silent retreat often enough. I knew I needed to keep releasing these distractions and stay on the path. Several times I found myself doubting whether I should even be there with so much work to do to prepare for the fall. A wiser voice rose up in the midst: *what better preparation than this?*

If we can stay with the practice, we will notice the thoughts as they rise. When we do, we can make sure they don't take root, notice when our mind wanders and bring it back to center. We drop down beneath into a wide expanse of stillness.

On the evening of the second day, something broke me open. I began to weep and I recognized this as the moment my defenses went down. I finally softened into this grace. The desert monks tell us that these tears are a gift, they signal an opening, a willingness to receive, a desire to be shaped.

By day three, I felt a marked shift in my prayer. I sat in spiritual direction and at the end of our time my retreat guide asked me, "What is your purpose?" Not what I do for work, but what is my deeper purpose as a human being in this life? Pilgrimage brings us intimately in touch with this question.

I went on a long hike on a hot and humid day. Thankfully, the forest provided some relief as I hiked into the beauty of the silent woods, not a single person around. The only company with me came in the form of a pair of deer and ants scrambling over the ground.

As I climbed the hills, I could feel my heart beat hard in my chest, and I relished the experience of being alive. After about an hour, it was time to turn back so that I wouldn't be late for evening meditation. I descended to the end of the trail and found a water trough with free-flowing, ice-cold water.

I stood, hot and sweaty from the exertion, under the bright blue sunlit sky. My hands trembled as I plunged them in the pool of water and felt enlivened by the gift. I drank thirstily to quench myself. I splashed the water on my head and blessed myself. I felt alive and grateful. I felt at home in the world.

I returned for silent meditation, feeling the exhilaration of the journey. As I settled into the quiet, the retreat director's question about my purpose came to me. A phrase shimmered forth in response: *"Drink freely of the life you have been given."*

I settled into meditation, savoring the gift of cold mountain water at the end of a long, hot hike. This moment resembled my life: the call to become willing to receive freely the gift of refreshment so generously offered to me.

Ten minutes into our half hour of prayer, I heard the sound of rain beginning to fall outside on the roof. By the time prayer finished and we went to dinner, the sky poured forth water. The storm seemed to come out of nowhere. I felt like God was saying, "See, there is not just a fountain to drink from but an abundance being offered to you." When we arrive home again, we discover that life is fuller than we had ever noticed before.

After dinner, as the rain subsided, I went out to dance barefoot in the wet grass in celebration.

The rest of my retreat broke open this invitation, this "word" I had received in prayer:

"Drink freely" meant not to hold back, to allow myself to be quenched, and to give myself over to the offering. Those voices of criticism and judgment are just ways we hold ourselves back from receiving

the fullness being offered. When we do, we reject the generous love of God.

The call taught me to consider all the ways I reject this love and how the inner voices of criticism keep me from the deep call of my heart. It is amazing how hard we work to keep ourselves from freedom.

"*. . . of the life you have been given,*" meaning the one, brilliant, beautiful, and unique experience of being me in this moment of time. I went back to the poet Rilke and his invitation to savor the inner landscape of our lives. He calls us to recognize that we are here to experience the fullness of ourselves in ache and in joy. We are to welcome in the entirety of our person. This is what coming home is about.

This phrase seems so basic and something I already knew. In other ways, I am struck by how hard it is to live a life of not holding ourselves back from God. We also seem to avoid giving ourselves over to the gift of our wondrous experience.

Each day on the retreat, in the morning and evening, we lit a small fire as part of our ritual of reminding ourselves that another twelve hours had passed. The director asked us repeated questions: *What choices had we made? How would we live this next twelve hours? How will I drink freely in the hours to come?*

How quickly we fall asleep again and again to this truth, that life is extraordinarily precious. Each is a unique expression of the divine, and there is the paradox that within the felt limits of chronological time, there is a generosity beyond our imagining pouring forth life into us. The question becomes: *How do we stay awake? How do we drink freely and abundantly? How do we stop holding back? How do we embrace the home within us that calls us to return?*

Once I returned back home to the rhythm of ordinary life, I kept struggling to remember those moments of beauty, to feel their gravity in my bones. So much conspires to make me forget, so many thoughts want me to hold back. This is being a pilgrim: to stay committed to awakening each moment to the truth of life's generosity. I'm to give myself over to the immense love beating through me. I'm to allow it to spill over into everything I do and with everyone I meet.

Every threshold in life is an invitation to this kind of rededication. As we cross over into something new, we pause, we commit ourselves anew.

How will you sing a rededication of your own life as we come to the end of this pilgrimage and retreat? How will you remind yourself of this in the days to come? How are you being called home again?

Reflection by John Valters Paintner

THE STORY OF THE ROAD TO EMMAUS (LK 24:13–35)

The same day that Mary of Magdalene, Joanna, and Mary the mother of James found the empty tomb, two other disciples made a seven-mile journey from the city of Jerusalem to the village of Emmaus.

Along the way, they encountered Jesus (though they did not recognize Him). He asked them what they had been discussing and so the disciples began to explain to Jesus all that had happened. They went through the arrest of Jesus, the trial, his execution, and that his tomb had just been found to be empty.

Jesus explained to the two how all that the scriptures and prophets foretold about the *messiah* had been fulfilled in Jesus. The disciples, amazed at what Jesus said, invited him to stay with them in Emmaus that night. At table, Jesus took the bread, blessed it, and gave it to the disciples. Finally their eyes opened and they recognized Jesus in the breaking of the bread. Jesus vanished from their sight.

Their hearts fired up at all that Jesus revealed to them in scripture and in the breaking of the bread. The two set out at once to return to Jerusalem. When they got back from Emmaus, the two disciples found the eleven Apostles and retold all that they had experienced. They all started to believe that Christ rose and was with them.

REFLECTION ON THE ROAD TO EMMAUS

It's unclear from the gospel account why the two disciples were going to Emmaus. We don't even know that much about them. Only one of them is named, a man named Cleopas. Classical artistic expressions of this gospel story tend to depict two men walking, talking, and eating with Jesus.

However, the fact that the second disciple is not named may indicate that the other disciple was a woman, perhaps Cleopas' wife. (No real "proof," per se, but an added level of possible reflection to be sure.)

About the only thing we can be sure about these two disciples on the road to Emmaus is that they certainly weren't expecting to encounter the risen Jesus. They did not even recognize him until they stopped to share a meal together. While their hearts burned as Jesus revealed to them the interpretation of scripture, it wasn't until Jesus broke bread with them that everything became known.

Did they not "see" Jesus because he was in disguise until the time was right? Or did their own expectations about the world keep them from seeing what was actually before them?

Yet the reason behind the delay in the two disciples recognizing Jesus in their midst isn't really the most pressing issue. The greater significance came from the immediate reactions of the two disciples to this amazing discovery. After recovering from the initial shock, the two ran back home immediately to share all that they had learned. They couldn't wait to share their experience on the road to Emmaus with others they'd left behind.

Much has been written about the classical "hero's journey" and how it usually ends with the hero's return home with a gift to be shared. These two disciples are true heroes in that sense. Why they were on the road to Emmaus in the first place becomes insignificant when they discover God in their midst. So they return home to share the Good News with those they knew and loved.

INVITATION TO LECTIO: THE ROAD TO EMMAUS (LK 24:31–35)

> With that their eyes were opened and they recognized him, but he vanished from their sight. Then they said to each other, "Were not our hearts burning [within us] while he spoke to us on the way and opened the scriptures to us?" So they set out at once and returned to Jerusalem where they found gathered together the eleven and those with them who were saying, "The Lord has truly been raised and has appeared to Simon!" Then the two recounted

what had taken place on the way and how he was made known to
them in the breaking of the bread.

WRITING EXPLORATION THROUGH MIDRASH

Our scripture text is the story of the Road to Emmaus at the moment of
revelation that Jesus had been walking alongside the two disciples all along.

Begin by finding a quiet space, connect to your breath, and sink into
stillness. As you settle in, be present to what you are feeling as we near
the end of this pilgrimage together. Notice without trying to change it,
just allow yourself to feel whatever you are experiencing. Rest into the
truth of how you find yourself.

Then step into the story and see what you encounter first through
your senses. Welcome in taste, touch, sound, smell, and what you see
before you. Be present in the walking; see what it feels like to not know
at first that Jesus is by your side. Explore the moment of your own revelation and discovery to know that the divine was with you all along.
Know yourself at home in that moment.

Notice if there are missing pieces to the story you want to fill in from
your imagination. Engage in dialogue with those present, asking for wisdom about returning back home again on your own pilgrimage journey.

When you have come to a place of rest, allow some time to record
your discoveries.

MIDRASH EXPLORATIONS

Hello! My name is Benjamin—Ben—for short. I live in Emmaus,
a small village in Canaan. I have a wonderful master called Cleopas, he tells me I'm his best friend, and if you've not guessed it
already, I'm a dog. I belong to the Canaan breed of dogs, and we
have a proud history of working with shepherds and their sheep
in this region for centuries. Cleopas has a small flock and I love
going out, helping him to round them up.

But enough about me! I'm back in the farmhouse now. Aliza,
wife of Cleopas, suddenly bursts into the room, and is telling her
daughter Ruth, about an extraordinary experience she and Joseph
have just had on the road from Jerusalem. I jump up and move
out of the way, all ears!

"Your Dad and I are walking home," Aliza says. "A stranger joins us who seems to know all about what's been going on in Jerusalem last weekend. We tell him what a great tragedy and disappointment the death of Jesus has been. And we go on . . . 'We had such great hopes in Jesus. It seems the bottom has dropped out of life since he died.' The stranger says nothing."

"What's his name? " asks Ruth.

"D'y'know," says Aliza, "I was in such a whirl, I didn't think of asking. But as we go along, I feel extraordinary warmth around us, a kind of mystical glow, and when he looks at me he seems to see straight into my heart. I decide we must ask him here for a meal, so I have run on ahead so we can get things ready. Now come on Ruth, they'll be here soon."

As for me—Ben—I'm intrigued at what I'm hearing. Dogs can always sniff it out when there's something strange in the air! I hear footsteps, and rush to meet Cleopas and the stranger. Woof! Woof! Yes! What a man! . . . What a presence! His eyes seem to caress me, even me—a dog—before I ever reach him. Then he strokes his hands around my neck and on my face. It's like nothing I've ever felt before. They come in. I'm in a dream . . . "Ben," I hear the voice of Cleopas calling. "Come on in . . . sit."

After introducing the stranger to Ruth, Cleopas offers a thanksgiving and the meal and conversation begin. The stranger's voice is so calm and gentle—kindness itself! I can tell he's really special, I'd almost say "out of this world." Animals understand more than they let on sometimes. My tail is wagging at all the excitement, and you never know, I might get a few titbits!

Now comes something I shall never forget. The stranger takes a loaf of bread. I saw Ruth bake it this morning. He breaks it . . . . There's a silence. I've never "heard" one like it before! Cleopas and Aliza look at each other. "IT'S JESUS!" they exclaim, stretching their arms towards him. And as if that isn't enough miracle for one day, I blink, paw both eyes . . . and he's not there . . . disappeared . . . evaporated into thin air. The room remains silent for a l-o-n-g time. Aliza and Ruth are in tears, Cleopas has his head in his hands. I go outside for some fresh air. I do believe my own eyes have a slight moistness about them. But look! One of those sheep has got out. After it Ben!

—James Sargent

There was no warmth by the fire. The flames couldn't penetrate the cold we had absorbed. And so we took to the road, heads down. It seemed less vulnerable that way. Draw no attention. To be visible in Jerusalem was questionable. Even a few miles might help. We walked in silence. No words could repair the wide breach events had opened. What lay ahead? One foot and then another. Is he fleeing too? I don't remember him. Who is he? Perhaps we should be careful. Don't say too much! But there is a thawing around my heart and a welcome when he speaks. My fear softens. Dare we share bread?

—**Rev. Dr. Martha Brunell**

CREATIVE EXPLORATION THROUGH PHOTOGRAPHY

For our final chapter, I invite you onto one last contemplative walk as an intentional part of your pilgrimage journey. Hold the story of the Road to Emmaus in your heart and be present as you walk to the ways that God is present to you even when you are not aware.

Bring your camera along and be open to receive images which shimmer with this truth. Pay attention to moments which speak to you of "home," whatever that might mean for you at this point in the pilgrimage. You are not trying to figure this out, but let the world offer you its symbols and images and then listen for what they might offer to you.

CLOSING BLESSING

The pilgrimage continues on for each of us. The discovery of the home within is something we must continue learning.

We sometimes think of the journey as a linear path to travel, when in reality we travel more in circles and spirals. We don't arrive at the summit and proclaim ourselves. We arrive back at the desires which set us on the path in the first place but perhaps with deeper wisdom or more doubts this time around.

Pilgrimage leads us home again, but that home is deep within each of us. We will cycle through our lives, meeting old themes, being invited to release, to walk forward in trust, to embrace mystery many times.

I offer you a closing poem to bless the circle of pilgrims you've joined by reading and engaging with this book, as well as the great circle of your lives which carry you forward.

In Praise of Circles

> I live my life in growing orbits which move out
> over this wondrous world.
>
> —**Rainer Maria Rilke**, *Book of Hours*

Friends around the dinner table
their mouths making "o's of delight and laughter,
plates piled with new potatoes, pearl onions, and pork loin.

Time softens the edges of river stones,
the arc of waves reach for shore,
celestial orbiting spheres keep cosmic time.

There is the saffron yolk, blood oranges, and blueberries,
the coins in my purse that let me buy fresh meat and
vegetables, a steaming bowl of bone broth.

St. Hildegard of Bingen saw the universe as a cosmic egg,
and St. Francis of Assisi displayed those wounds in his
palms,
icons halo their heads with gold.

The mossy green iris of my lover's eyes, lost together
in a circle of mingled limbs, breasts and bellies, imperfect,
soft, and round. The ring he slid on my finger years ago.

The curve of the old woman's back bent over from
a thousand griefs. The pregnant belly ripening.
Blood ebbing and flowing through our bodies.

Monks arising for prayers, entering
the great cycle of rising and falling,
Sufi dervishes whirling, always left around the heart.

We say "going in circles" when we mean nowhere.

Why do we worship the straight lines,
the most direct route, nonstop, leaving the past far behind?

A circle is both diameter and circumference,
compass and horizon, holding center and edge together,
calling us to the heart and the wild borders.

Winter's fierce stripping away will always come again,
but so will dahlias and desire. Memories unbidden, circle
around like birds returning from migration.

The journey isn't just the steep ascent up the holy mountain,
but the descent back to the daily, those friends still
lingering by the fire, the bottle of wine now lying empty.

CONCLUSION

There is a wonderful poem by Mary Oliver titled, "Almost a Conversation" in which she describes her encounter with an otter who does not want a computer or a dry home but wonders, "morning after morning, that river is so cold and fresh and alive, and still/I don't jump in."[1]

This is the call of pilgrimage, to dive into the waters of life and see where the current carries us.

My own life pilgrimage experience so far has been both the delight of following the otter's invitation and also making friends with the fierce winds that blow here in Ireland. This wind which comes in off the Atlantic, which I want so much to resist, asks me to stay and allow myself to be slowly carved.

This is definitely an ongoing journey. I alternate between the exhilaration of knowing I've truly followed my heart these last years and the grief of both letting go and being in a deep, unknowing place. I continue to be on a threshold. I have caught glimpses of this woman who is myself, who is carved by the wind and does not resist swimming in the rushing river.

Pilgrimage is about diving in and not holding back. It's about running headlong toward your deepest desire, which always awaits you with open arms. I imagine those ancient monks and pilgrims who knew this longing as well. They yearned for an experience of God beyond the boundaries of what they had known. They let this desire lead them to wild edges.

What continues to be the deepest wisdom for me is the call to release my effort, the summons to fall into the embrace of the One who offers an abundance of nourishment. I'm learning to trust in the unfinished nature of things. This calls me to give my heart to my work, as I always strive to do, and then wrap myself in the shawl of humility to honor my own limitations. Can I allow myself to simply sink into this moment, rest, and receive the fruit?

I wish the same for you, my beloved pilgrim readers: to be ever so gentle with yourself, knowing that life calls us to the twin path of jumping whole-heartedly and surrendering ourselves into an ocean of care. When we do, we are guaranteed support so that we move through the world well-nourished.

May you jump right into that great river, so fresh and alive.

ACKNOWLEDGMENTS

Every book is the unseen collaboration of countless sources of support. I am always deeply grateful to my husband, John, for being on this life pilgrimage with me, offering me unflagging support in this creative path, and for sharing his wisdom and insight into the scripture stories in these pages.

Thanks always goes to Ave Maria Press for being such enthusiastic supporters of my writing, and especially to Bob Hamma for being flexible with some project deadlines. Thanks to Jonathan Ryan for his good work on editing and helping to refine the writing for publication.

I also want to thank the amazing community of dancing monks that is Abbey of the Arts. What started as a humble blog has now become a community of thousands, many of whom have joined us on pilgrimages in Ireland, Germany, and Austria. This work has unfolded on its own journey of discovery, and I love the fellow pilgrims I have encountered along the way. I am particularly grateful to those who participated in the two online courses which eventually became the material for this book and to those who generously shared their Midrash explorations for inclusion in these pages.

ACKNOWLEDGMENTS

NOTES

Introduction

1. For more about the practice of lectio divina and the practice of contemplative photography, see *Lectio Divina—The Sacred Art: Transforming Words and Images into Heart-Centered Prayer* by Christine Valters Paintner (published by SkyLight Paths) and *Eyes of the Heart: Photography as a Contemplative Practice* by Christine Valters Paintner (published by Ave Maria Press).

1. The Practice of Hearing the Call and Responding

1. Thomas Merton, *New Seeds of Contemplation* (New York: New Directions Books, 2007), 31–32.

3. The Practice of Crossing the Threshold

1. Benedicta Ward, trans., *The Sayings of the Desert Fathers: The Alphabetical Collection* (Collegeville, MN: Liturgical Press, 1984), 83.

2. Gregory Mayers, *Listen to the Desert: Secrets of Spiritual Maturity from the Desert Fathers and Mothers* (Liguori, MO: Liguori Publications, 1996), 50.

3. David Adam, *Border Lands: The Best of David Adam's Celtic Vision* (Lanham, MD: Sheed & Ward, 1999), Kindle edition.

4. The Practice of Making the Way by Walking

1. Ray Simpson, *Exploring Celtic Spirituality: Historic Roots for Our Future* (London: Hodder & Stoughton Religious, 1999).

5. THE PRACTICE OF BEING UNCOMFORTABLE

1. Belden C. Lane, *The Solace of Fierce Landscapes: Exploring Desert and Mountain Spirituality* (New York: Oxford University Press, 2007), 20.

2. Carl Jung, *Memories, Dreams, Reflections*, ed. Aniela Jaffe and trans. Clara Winston and Richard Winston (New York: Vintage Books, 1989), 358.

3. Barbara Brown Taylor, *An Altar in the World: A Geography of Faith* (New York: HarperOne, 2010), 69.

4. Thomas Merton, *Life and Prayer: Journey in Christ* (New York: Electronic Paperbacks).

6. THE PRACTICE OF BEGINNING AGAIN

1. Ward, *Sayings of the Desert Fathers*, 224.

7. THE PRACTICE OF EMBRACING THE UNKNOWN

1. Carl Jung to M. Leonard, December 1959.

2. Alan W. Jones, *Soul Making: The Desert Way of Spirituality* (New York: HarperOne, 1989), 26.

3. Simone Weil, *Gravity and Grace* (London: Routledge Classics, 2002), 114.

4. Ward, *Sayings of the Desert Fathers*, 4.

CONCLUSION

1. Mary Oliver, "Almost a Conversation," in *Evidence: Poems* (Boston: Beacon Press, 2010), 30.

Christine Valters Paintner is the online abbess for Abbey of the Arts (abbey-ofthearts.com), a virtual monastery offering classes and resources on contemplative practice and creative expression. She holds a doctorate in Christian spirituality from the Graduate Theological Union in Berkeley, California, and earned her professional status as a registered expressive arts consultant and educator from the International Expressive Arts Therapy Association.

Paintner is the author of *The Eyes of the Heart*; *Water, Wind, Earth, and Fire*; and *The Artist's Rule* and is a columnist for the progressive Christian portal at Patheos. She leads pilgrimages in Ireland, Austria, and Germany, and online retreats at her website, living out her commitment as a Benedictine Oblate in Galway, Ireland, with her husband John.

AVE

Ave Maria Press

Founded in 1865, Ave Maria Press,
a ministry of the Congregation of
Holy Cross, is a Catholic publishing
company that serves the spiritual and
formative needs of the Church and its
schools, institutions, and ministers;
Christian individuals and families; and
others seeking spiritual nourishment.

For a complete listing of titles from

Ave Maria Press

Sorin Books

Forest of Peace

Christian Classics

visit www.avemariapress.com

AVE MARIA PRESS
Notre Dame, IN
A Ministry of the United States Province of Holy Cross